New Daylight

Edited by Sally Welch

May–August 2016

New Daylight © BRF 2016

The Bible Reading Fellowship
15 The Chambers, Vineyard, Abingdon OX14 3FE
Tel: 01865 319700; Fax: 01865 319701
E-mail: enquiries@brf.org.uk; Website: www.brf.org.uk

ISBN 978 0 85746 391 3

Distributed in Australia by Mediacom Education Inc., PO Box 610, Unley, SA 5061.
Tel: 1800 811 311; Fax: 08 8297 8719;
E-mail: admin@mediacom.org.au
Available also from all good Christian bookshops in Australia.
For individual and group subscriptions in Australia:
Mrs Rosemary Morrall, PO Box W35, Wanniassa, ACT 2903.

Distributed in New Zealand by Scripture Union Wholesale, PO Box 760, Wellington
Tel: 04 385 0421; Fax: 04 384 3990; E-mail: suwholesale@clear.net.nz

Publications distributed to more than 60 countries

Acknowledgments

Printed by Gutenberg Press, Tarxien, Malta.

Suggestions for using *New Daylight*

Find a regular time and place, if possible, where you can read and pray undistracted. Before you begin, take time to be still and perhaps use the BRF prayer. Then read the Bible passage slowly (try reading it aloud if you find it over-familiar), followed by the comment. You can also use *New Daylight* for group study and discussion, if you prefer.

The prayer or point for reflection can be a starting point for your own meditation and prayer. Many people like to keep a journal to record their thoughts about a Bible passage and items for prayer. In *New Daylight* we also note the Sundays and some special festivals from the Church calendar, to keep in step with the Christian year.

New Daylight and the Bible

New Daylight contributors use a range of Bible versions, and you will find a list of the versions used opposite, on page 2. You are welcome to use your own preferred version alongside the passage printed in the notes. This can be particularly helpful if the Bible text has been abridged.

New Daylight affirms that the whole of the Bible is God's revelation to us, and we should read, reflect on and learn from every part of both Old and New Testaments. Usually the printed comment presents a straightforward 'thought for the day', but sometimes it may also raise questions rather than simply providing answers, as we wrestle with some of the more difficult passages of Scripture.

New Daylight is also available in a deluxe edition (larger format). Visit your local Christian bookshop or contact the BRF office, who can also give details about a cassette version for the visually impaired. For a Braille edition, contact St John's Guild, Sovereign House, 12–14 Warwick Street, Coventry CV5 6ET.

Comment on *New Daylight*

To send feedback, you may email or write to BRF at the addresses shown opposite. If you would like your comment to be included on our website, please email connect@brf.org.uk. You can also Tweet to @brfonline, using the hashtag #brfconnect.

Writers in this issue

Rachel Boulding is Deputy Editor of the *Church Times*. She was previously Senior Liturgy Editor at Church House Publishing. She lives in Dorset with her husband and son—and, during school terms, more than 70 teenage boys.

Helen Julian CSF is an Anglican Franciscan sister, currently serving her community as Minister General. She has written three books for BRF, including *Living the Gospel* and *The Road to Emmaus*.

Stephen Rand is a writer and speaker who worked with Tearfund for many years, and then Open Doors, travelling widely. He now helps lead Fresh Streams—a largely Baptist church leaders' network.

Michael Mitton is a freelance writer, speaker and consultant and the Fresh Expressions Adviser for the Derby Diocese. He is also the NSM Priest-in-charge of St Paul's Derby. He is the author of *Dreaming of Home* (BRF, 2012) and *Travellers of the Heart* (BRF, 2013).

Penelope Wilcock writes Christian fiction, pastoral theology and Bible study. Her books include *Spiritual Care of Dying and Bereaved People* (BRF, 2013). She blogs at http://kindredofthequietway.blogspot.co.uk.

Andrew Jones is Archdeacon of Meirionnydd in the Diocese of Bangor. He has written *Pilgrimage: the journey to remembering our story* (BRF, 2011) and *Mary: a Gospel witness to transfiguration and liberation* (BRF, 2014).

Sally Welch is a parish priest in the Diocese of Oxford. She has written several books on aspects of adults' and children's spirituality and has a particular interest in pilgrimage and labyrinths.

Harry Smart is an Anglican priest and has been a mental and general hospital chaplain for many years. He has an interest in mindfulness and in labyrinths and has used them for patient and staff support. He lives in north Lincolnshire.

Veronica Zundel is an Oxford graduate, writer and journalist. She lives with her husband and son in North London, where they belong to the Mennonite Church. She has written *Everything I Know about God I've Learned from Being a Parent* (BRF, 2013).

Sally Welch writes...

I always think it rather a shame that the Church calls so much of its calendar Ordinary Time! Surely there must be a better word for describing the long chain of days that links the summer months, when the landscape surrounding us is growing into green maturity, the daylight lingers long into the evening and even the rain has a different quality to that of the more demanding winter weather? Thankfully, the contributions we have put together for this issue will enable us to nourish our spiritual roots, drawing inspiration and support from the thought-provoking words and reflections that are offered here, helping us to grow and develop in our relationship with God.

In the light of this hope, it may seem strange to begin this issue with Rachel Boulding's remarkable and moving thoughts on 'Facing death', but the time between the Ascension of Christ and Pentecost (15 May) is a liminal time when we are more than ever aware of the 'now' and the 'not yet'—a feeling that will be familiar to those who have faced or are facing life-threatening illnesses. The reassurance of Pentecost and the blessing of the Holy Spirit brings joy and hope to Christians today, just as it did to those first, frightened apostles, huddled in an upper room in Jerusalem so long ago. Sister Helen Julian's description of the life of Brigid reminds us of the long line of faithful believers linking us to those first disciples as we try to follow in Christ's footsteps. In this we are helped, as Brigid also must have been, by the advice given to us by Paul and John in their letters to the faithful members of the early church. These letters, filled with love and encouraging, can be a great support to communities and individuals struggling with 'being church' today. The relevance of these letters, and the Gospels themselves, to the issues of today is explored in the contributions of Penelope Wilcock and Harry Smart, which focus on the subject of feasting and fasting in the New Testament, partnering our study of those subjects in the Old Testament in the previous issue.

I hope you find this issue provides you with much sustenance for your spiritual journey this summer, making this time Extra Ordinary...

Sally Ann Welch

The BRF Prayer

Almighty God,
you have taught us that your word is a lamp for our feet
and a light for our path. Help us, and all who prayerfully
read your word, to deepen our fellowship with you
and with each other through your love.
And in so doing may we come to know you more fully,
love you more truly, and follow more faithfully
in the steps of your son Jesus Christ, who lives and reigns
with you and the Holy Spirit, one God for evermore.
Amen

Facing death

When I suggested writing something about my situation of having terminal cancer, the kind editors at BRF encouraged me, saying that it would be useful to hear from someone going through the middle of a particular experience—rather than what others might think about it from the outside. So many of us Christians are eager to chip in with ideas about what others ought to be doing or feeling or what they think the Bible says about a subject that sometimes the heart of what it feels like gets lost. There can be something valuable in hearing about the experience from the inside, right now as it is happening.

Often big events in life, such as bereavement or serious illness, are hard to imagine beforehand. They can feel very different from what we had expected, as well as being varied in people's varied circumstances. So I have tried to be as honest as I can, even when it involves bewilderment and uncertainty.

For some people, I realise, these big experiences lead to serious questioning of their beliefs or even a loss of faith. While I would always try to respect what they are going through, that has not been the case for me. Through no effort or merit of my own, I have found this to be an oddly unexpected time of blessing. Perhaps I am being naïve, but I really am trying to be true to what has happened and how it has struck me, not just write what decent Christians might wish to hear.

So I have tried to go through some of the various aspects of facing a life-limiting illness as they have occurred to me in terms of what such things can mean, both for the person who is dying and for those around him or her. This is not a linear progression with tightly defined stages, but a matter of varied facets coming into view at particular times, then fading away, only to return—often in a slightly different way. In some respects, this is similar to the experience of bereavement.

In all of this, I have tried to frame my thoughts in the context of all life being a gift from God, to be celebrated in the light of his grace and love for each one of us.

RACHEL BOULDING

Disbelief and denial

Lord, let me know mine end, and the number of my days: that I may be certified how long I have to live. Behold, thou hast made my days as it were a span long: and mine age is even as nothing in respect of thee; and verily every man living is altogether vanity. For man walketh in a vain shadow, and disquieteth himself in vain: he heapeth up riches, and cannot tell who shall gather them. And now, Lord, what is my hope: truly my hope is even in thee.

'I can't believe this is happening.' A diagnosis of cancer—or any life-threatening disease—often seems inherently unbelievable. If I am the person who is ill, I cannot get my head round it, nor can those around me. They struggle to make sense of what is being said and cannot believe that they have heard correctly.

Some people try to block it out—'This absolutely cannot be happening. I'm too young and I don't even feel unwell' or 'The doctors must be wrong: she looks fine and has a healthy lifestyle.' It seems as if something in human nature, especially in modern Western society, simply cannot grasp the idea of terminal illness as a personal experience. It might be an event in films or books, something that happens to other people, but not to me or those I love.

Why should it not happen to me, though? I know that people do die of diseases before they reach the average span of eighty-something, so why not me? OK, I am not a smoker, not obese, but all sorts of people get cancer.

When I was first diagnosed with secondary breast cancer—a return of the disease, which has now spread to various parts of my body—the idea of dying early played around in my head, coming round and back in a way that was like the experience of grief. Sometimes now, too, I can accept that it is happening, but often it seems like a bad dream from which I hope to wake.

Loving Father, draw me towards you and the truth of your complete knowledge of me. Help me to realise that I exist in you; my life is hidden in yours, however long it might be. Amen

RACHEL BOULDING

Processing the information

So if you have been raised with Christ, seek the things that are above, where Christ is, seated at the right hand of God. Set your minds on things that are above, not on things that are on earth, for you have died, and your life is hidden with Christ in God. When Christ who is your life is revealed, then you also will be revealed with him in glory.

Part of the process of facing up to life-threatening illness is the difficulty of absorbing a great deal of information in a relatively short time. Much of the news is technical—medical, even financial—and emotional. It would be hard to take in if I was studying it in an abstract sense or had time to take it all in, but the huge fact is that it is happening to me, right now.

There are so many different and new ideas that I do not understand, especially about treatments. I am neither a doctor nor a psychologist. It is just too much to take in, especially when I am not feeling 100 per cent and am full of anxiety about the future. I cannot grasp what any of this might mean for me.

In some ways, this is an extension of the seemingly endless circles of denial that I wrote about yesterday. It is too complicated, so it cannot be happening. I think it is important not to pretend that this bafflement is anything but hardgoing and enduring. It will not be shaken off with a bright suggestion of 'You've got to be positive.' Yes, it can be offered up in prayer—this is something we can all try, even when we feel alone and God understands pain, confusion and abandonment from the inside, having suffered on the cross.

None of this is going to be easy. We need to dig deep into our trust in God and our knowledge of his blessings. Then we might have a fuller sense of his grace, which will more thoroughly equip us to face the current confusion and look to the future with hope.

Heavenly Father, I cannot believe what is happening or take in what it means. Help me to hold on to a mustard seed of faith in you, even in the deepest darkness, which may grow to a fuller understanding of your constant love for me. Amen

RACHEL BOULDING

Anger and envy—and trust

Trust in the Lord with all your heart, and do not rely on your own insight. In all your ways acknowledge him, and he will make straight your paths. Do not be wise in your own eyes; fear the Lord, and turn away from evil. It will be a healing for your flesh and a refreshment for your body.

The denial and dazed bewilderment of life-threatening illness never seem to go away completely, churning round in circles of variations on a theme, but other thoughts often sneak up on me, too. If I do not watch out, I find myself wondering what I have done to deserve this. The sense of 'Why *not* me?'—the knowledge that I have no more merit than anyone else, whether others are obese smokers or not—can get lost.

The fact is that illnesses happen in this world and can take anyone away before what they might think is their rightful span. Yes, we can contribute to our risk of dying, such as by binge drinking or driving dangerously, but mostly it is more a matter of 'Stuff happens.'

Still, I find myself looking enviously at the over-sixties when I realise I will never see that decade for myself. People may be elderly and frail, but at least they are alive. There is another way of looking at this, too. Why are we all not more concerned about helping older people face death? Why should people feel so sorry for me and wonder how I am going to cope with dying in my fifties when there are so many more people going through something similar in their later decades? Surely we should be doing much, much more to think about something that we all have to go through.

In a way (and I have to be careful how I put this, to avoid seeming to revel in the shock factor and goriness of it all), it is a privilege to have a chance to contemplate such matters with an earlier end in sight. It concentrates the mind and helps to undermine some of the inevitable denial, so that I can focus on what really counts.

Lord God of the universe, lead me into your ways and away from the twisted paths of self-righteousness and envy.

RACHEL BOULDING

In the context of God's grace

Ho, everyone who thirsts, come to the waters; and you that have no money, come, buy and eat!... Why do you spend your money for that which is not bread, and your labour for that which does not satisfy?... Incline your ear, and come to me; listen, so that you may live. I will make with you an everlasting covenant, my steadfast, sure love for David.

At such points of feeling battered by the maelstrom of emotions, fear, confusing information and bewilderment, it is easy to lose sight of what really matters and the true state of the universe. The fact is that God has created the world and each one of us and we exist to love him and reflect his love to others. He invites every individual to share abundant life in him and it is up to us how we respond.

Whether I have decades of life ahead or only a few weeks, months or years, there are things I can do, right now, to say 'Yes' to what he offers and bask in the warmth of his grace. It is about making the most of what I have.

Yes, there is a time to grieve for a future I might not have and the loss of experiences I might be looking forward to, but there is so much that I can do now, whatever might happen. I can enjoy God's gifts, right here. As Denise Inge, the Christian scholar, wrote when she knew she was dying in her early fifties, 'The cancer has not made life more precious—that would make it seem like something fragile to lock away in the cupboard. No, it has made it more delicious' (*A Tour of Bones*, Continuum, 2014).

This is not a case of pretending that the grief and anxiety have gone away; it is more a case of needing to realise they are not the whole picture. Sometimes, it is useful to remind myself of this, perhaps with deep breaths and words such as the Jesus Prayer: 'Lord Jesus Christ, Son of the Living God, have mercy on me, a sinner.'

Loving Father, help me to see beyond my immediate fears
and to know that you are alongside me, whether or not
I sense you.

RACHEL BOULDING

In uncertainty: seek the Lord

Seek the Lord while he may be found, call upon him while he is near; let the wicked forsake their way, and the unrighteous their thoughts; let them return to the Lord, that he may have mercy on them, and to our God, for he will abundantly pardon. For my thoughts are not your thoughts, nor are your ways my ways, says the Lord.

Facing life-threatening illness is part of a delicate, often fragile balance, which constantly needs to be renegotiated. It is between, on the one hand, some sort of realism about the medical facts—the way that the cancer has spread in my body—and, on the other, the sense that I am not giving up and deciding to die. I trust in the Lord, live in hope and try to make the most of what I have. This can be true whether I might have only weeks to live and be in a frail state or I am feeling well and have years ahead.

Often, it is the uncertainty that seems most difficult. It can seem debilitating, making planning impossible, and even thinking about the future seem fraught with danger. If we all knew how long we had on this planet, we fantasise that we would know securely where we were, we would be able to map out the time ahead and everything would be fine and dandy, but this is only a dream. There are so many things we can never know and we had better get used to it.

So we can make the most of the opportunities we have and relish each day and moment of blessing. As Denise Inge wrote, 'Contemplating mortality is not about being prepared to die, it is about being prepared to live… Living is not something outside you that you will do one day when you have organised your life a little better. It comes from deep in the centre of yourself. You have to let the life in, there at the deepest part, and live it from the inside out.'

I believe in the sun, even when it doesn't shine. I believe in love, even when I don't feel it. I believe in God, even when he is silent.

Written by German Jews suffering Nazi persecution
RACHEL BOULDING

When those fears come back

Hear my prayer, O Lord, and with thine ears consider my calling: hold not thy peace at my tears. For I am a stranger with thee: and a sojourner, as all my fathers were. O spare me a little, that I may recover my strength: before I go hence, and be no more seen.

As I said earlier, the idea of facing death feels a bit like going through bereavement: it involves stages of denial, anger, regret, depression and, if you are really blessed, occasional elements of acceptance. 'Stages' feels like a misleading term, though, because of the way these aspects of grief do not follow a linear order: they come, go, return and overlap, several of them at the same time.

Despite my endless desire to wriggle out of confronting the big issues, I think it would be healthy to tackle my real fears about dying as honestly as I can. Anything else feels like ducking my responsibilities and the tremendous opportunity that all this presents to explore the fundamental truths of the life God has given us.

Many people are obviously worried by the process of dying—the potential for physical pain and the isolation of going away alone. There is also the revolting unpleasantness of bodily functions, smells and the indignity of being unable to take care of myself. None of this is surprising, because it is part of our essential humanity and our wish to live decently and keep parts of our self and our body private.

Strangely, though, the physical aspects do not happen to worry me so much. End-of-life palliative care is excellent now where I live in Britain—thanks partly to the work of Christians such as Cecily Saunders, the founder of the hospice movement. Medical members of staff are experts in managing pain and making people's last days as comfortable as possible. I might be being naïve and overly optimistic about this, but I do not see any point in creating anxiety where I feel none at the moment. No, my main source of worry is about those left behind, which I will come to tomorrow.

Loving Father, help me to face my fears clearly and to trust in your steadfast love. Amen

RACHEL BOULDING

The grief of those left behind

The king was deeply moved, and went up to the chamber over the gate, and wept; and as he went, he said, 'O my son Absalom, my son, my son Absalom! Would that I had died instead of you, O Absalom, my son, my son!' It was told Joab, 'The king is weeping and mourning for Absalom.' So the victory that day was turned into mourning for all the troops; for the troops heard that day, 'The king is grieving for his son.'

My friends will be sad and will miss me, but my closest family will suffer most—just as I would if any of them were to die. My son, who is now 16, will grow up without me. I might just about last until his early 20s, but he will go through the rest of his life without a mother. My husband will lose me after three decades of marriage and there will be a gap by his side, even if he remarries (which I do hope he will, for all our sakes). Another hope is that my mother, now 90, will die before me. She says she is working on it—bizarre though it is to put it like this. It will also be hard for my brothers. I know that if any of them died, I would feel as if I had had a limb amputated, as I have a deep, visceral sense of being someone with three big brothers. This is an essential part of me, which I can never change.

It is not that I am so wonderful as a wife, mother, daughter or sister, it is just that I am the one they are used to. This is me, with all my faults and blessings. If my experience with dead friends and family is anything to go by, they will miss the exasperating parts as much as the lovely ones. This does not seem fair on them and I only pray that they can turn to God and the love of others to find comfort and hope.

Loving Father, in their time of loneliness and grief, draw my family and friends to you and your grace. Help them to know your presence beside them. Amen

RACHEL BOULDING

The pitfalls of compassion

When Jesus saw her [Mary] weeping, and the Jews who came with her also weeping, he was greatly disturbed in spirit and deeply moved… Jesus began to weep. So the Jews said, 'See how he loved him!'… He cried with a loud voice, 'Lazarus, come out!' The dead man came out.

Sometimes it can seem as if the worst part about being seriously ill is others' reactions. Suddenly, everyone treats you differently and this can hurt. When people ask what they should say or do to help, I would suggest that the most important thing is to say or do *something* and not avoid the person who is ill. The most damaging approach you can take is to shut someone out. Much of this is similar to when someone has been bereaved.

Almost always, it is better to say anything, very briefly, rather than nothing at all. The paralysing fear of your saying the wrong or hurtful thing is as nothing compared to the other person's pain at being shunned. Many ill people will have heard it all before anyway and got used to ignoring unhelpful comments. So, well-wishers could start with a plain, 'I'm sorry to hear…', carry on to, 'Would it help for me to do X?' (where X is some specific task, such as a lift or practical help around the home) and perhaps end with, 'I'll be thinking of you' or 'praying for you', depending on the person.

The idea of what is right for that person, at that moment, is crucial. Try to listen to them, without leaping in with your own comments. When they are talking about their condition, a simple, 'Yes, I see' or, 'That must have been hard' can be more helpful than, 'That's like the time when I…'. It can also be useful to leave them an escape clause, such as, 'Maybe that's not where you are right now.'

For myself, I find that assurances about medical advances, brave fights, a positive attitude or 'You'll be fine' can be hard to hear, though I try not to resort to violence when people mention them. They mean well, but they cannot really know how I feel.

Father, help us to think of others in the light of your grace and have mercy on us all. Amen

RACHEL BOULDING

Resources for hope

Praised be the Lord daily: even the God who helpeth us, and poureth his benefits upon us. He is our God, even the God of whom cometh salvation: God is the Lord, by whom we escape death... Thy God hath sent forth strength for thee: stablish the thing, O God, that thou hast wrought in us.

In the midst of these inner conflicts, God continues to pour out his blessings on us. He offers a huge range of resources that can help us personally. Part of this is evident in the Christian tradition of a 'good death'. The idea may have gone out of fashion, partly due to our modern reluctance to face the ultimate reality and our over-reliance on medical advances to solve our problems, but the help is there. So we can turn to the example of Christians such as John Donne (1572–1631), the poet whose passionate sexual writing developed into equally passionate words of desire for God (see *New Daylight: January—April 2014* for notes I wrote about him).

Donne was praised by the people of his time for having fashioned a good death. This involved practical activities, public and private, including making a careful will and inviting his friends to say goodbye. He also commissioned a sculpture of himself for his grave, which is still in St Paul's Cathedral to this day.

It might seem overly morbid, but I love the bracing realism of the way he posed for an artist to draw him as a shrouded corpse for his tomb. He seemed to want to confront what his dead body would look like. Perhaps such a literal depiction helped to bring home to him what his own death would be like; then it could hold fewer terrors. It is the unknown that frightens us most. Having the chance to create a true-to-death image must have felt like a good opportunity to do this.

In his final sermon, known as 'Death's Duel', he began with the words above from Psalm 68: 'He is our God...'. The message was that the whole of life looks forward to the end: 'all our periods and transitions in this life are so many passages from death to death.'

Father, ground me in your strength and grace, right to the end.

RACHEL BOULDING

Looking to Jesus on the cross

The soldiers also mocked him, coming up and offering him sour wine, and saying, 'If you are the King of the Jews, save yourself!'... Then Jesus, crying with a loud voice, said, 'Father, into your hands I commend my spirit.' Having said this, he breathed his last. When the centurion saw what had taken place, he praised God and said, 'Certainly this man was innocent.'

As we read yesterday, John Donne's approach, revelling in the details of death, is a huge contrast to modern attitudes. Instead of seeing death as part of life, we now regard it as a weird, infinitely postponeable and unconnected horror in the distant future. Why can we not grasp that it is perfectly natural and will happen to us all? Who are we trying to kid? Fool ourselves we do, though, and modern Western society seems to encourage us to do so. We hide death away in hospitals and shield our children from it, so that it no longer seems like a normal part of life. This can foster only fear of its unfamiliarity and mystery.

Christians used to be encouraged to look specifically at Jesus' death as an example, drawing on the fact of his saving sacrifice to find positive aspects to the end of life, as well as looking to his approach to the process of his death. So, just as he did not flinch from death— despite the genuine fear he expressed in Gethsemane—and later gave up his spirit to his Father in a positive way, so Christians are spurred on to face their end squarely and to be mindful of it.

Sometimes the idea of meeting death eagerly and seeing it as a spiritual opportunity could veer towards the obsessive, but, at its best, it fostered a healthy honesty. The Gospels' descriptions of Jesus' sufferings also gave an immediate well of experience that Christians could draw on. They could set their own pain alongside his, secure in the knowledge that he had endured worse horrors, both physical and in terms of his abandonment by so many of those he loved.

Lord Jesus, you died to set me free from the terrors of death.
Help me to set my sufferings at the foot of your cross. Amen

RACHEL BOULDING

Torn between grief and hope

For since death came through a man, the resurrection of the dead comes also through a man. For as in Adam all die, so in Christ all will be made alive. But each in turn: Christ, the firstfruits; then, when he comes, those who belong to him. Then the end will come, when he hands over the kingdom to God the Father after he has destroyed all dominion, authority and power. For he must reign until he has put all his enemies under his feet. The last enemy to be destroyed is death.

Most vitally, Jesus has defeated death. He lives now and will raise us with him. Christians should never minimise or dismiss the suffering of death and the shattering grief it causes, yet our pain is mingled with hope. The frightening separation of the dead person from their earlier existence and those left behind when the one they had loved is taken from them is set alongside a wider picture (see 1 Corinthians 15:54–57, the reading for the day after tomorrow). It can be hard to sense it, but even if it is only faintly in the background, it is something we can grow to appreciate, even if this takes a long time.

Of course, a death usually feels like searing pain, a terrible ripping apart of the normal order of life—even if the person dying is full of years, after a contented life and a fine Christian. We will still miss that person terribly.

Shakespeare offers a lighthearted-but-serious version of this sense of being torn in *Twelfth Night* (Act 1, Scene V), when Feste, the clown or 'Fool', tries to jolt Olivia out of her sadness, as she has been mired too long in grief for her brother. He declares, 'I think his soul is in hell' to provoke her reaction. She says, 'I know his soul is in heaven, fool.' He replies, 'The more fool, madonna, to mourn for your brother's soul being in heaven.'

Loving Father, guide me through the mixture of hopes and fears as I look forward to the coming of your kingdom. Amen

RACHEL BOULDING

Realism in the face of the end

For a thousand years in thy sight are but as yesterday: seeing that is past as a watch in the night. As soon as thou scatterest them they are even as a sleep: and fade away suddenly like the grass... The days of our age are threescore years and ten; and though men be so strong that they come to fourscore years: yet is their strength then but labour and sorrow; so soon passeth it away, and we are gone... So teach us to number our days: that we may apply our hearts unto wisdom.

Another positive aspect of dying that we have lost is its public nature. In many places in earlier centuries, the deathbed was a busy place, with streams of visitors. People could say their goodbyes simply, familiar as they were with the process. Hospices do their best to support those who are dying, both on their premises and in people's own homes, but often this is a struggle against the prevailing culture of the medicalisation of death and the desire to separate it from natural human interaction.

Despite this, we still rightly praise those who speak publicly about death—such as the actor Lynda Bellingham, who was frank in 2014 about stopping her gruelling cancer treatment. She realised that prolonging it would give her only a little longer and that time would be ravaged by sickness, so she decided to go for quality rather than quantity and died soon afterwards. She was applauded by the Marie Curie charity for the benefit she brought to others by using 'the language of acceptance' so openly.

Obviously, different people are on different paths at various stages, but we really need to face up to the fact that there can come a point at which there is not much more that the doctors or we can do to keep us alive for much longer. As Lynda Bellingham said about stopping treatment, 'This is my way of taking back control. I'm not giving up, just being realistic.' At this stage, it can be better for everyone for the patient to spend their last days with family and friends, saying goodbye and preparing spiritually.

Father, help me to prepare for the wonders of your nearer love. Amen

RACHEL BOULDING

Between realism and positivity

When this perishable body puts on imperishability, and this mortal body puts on immortality, then the saying that is written will be fulfilled: 'Death has been swallowed up in victory.' 'Where, O death, is your victory? Where, O death, is your sting?' The sting of death is sin, and the power of sin is the law. But thanks be to God, who gives us the victory through our Lord Jesus Christ.

The most senior cancer doctor I have spoken to assured me that the most important factor in medical treatment is the patient's attitude. Some people can drive themselves towards death, but others carry on much longer if they have something or someone to live for. People of faith do fare better. Reliable research backs up the fact that religious believers really do last longer with life-limiting illnesses.

There is another side to all this, however. I can try to stay strong and summon up a sunny outlook, particularly if it helps those around me, yet I have to admit that I need to be realistic: I will die before too long. It is a balancing act between genuine hope and the need to find the positives on the one hand and, on the other, a true assessment of my medical condition.

It can sometimes strike a false note to say, 'I'm going to fight this' if disease has advanced so far in my body. Eventually, it will become a battle I can never win. What is more, couching it in these military terms can even make it feel like my fault for not trying hard enough— as if I am dying because I have failed to make enough effort. Being honest, though, I can say, 'I'm going to face this head on.' I can engage with the medical details and try to make my last days count.

There are positive steps that most of us can take. We can assure our family and friends of our love, thank people who have helped us, phone or write to others (one line on a card can be enough) and make our peace with God. Hospice staff members often report how patients have found resolution and fulfilment by taking such actions.

'My grace is sufficient for you, for power is made perfect in weakness'
(2 Corinthians 12:9).

RACHEL BOULDING

He shall be our guide unto death

Great is the Lord, and highly to be praised: in the city of our God, even upon his holy hill... God is well known in her palaces as a sure refuge... We wait for thy loving-kindness, O God: in the midst of thy temple... For this God is our God for ever and ever: he shall be our guide unto death.

Whether we are dying ourselves or bracing ourselves for the death of someone close to us, we can at least try to take some of the fear out of the process of departing. Ignorance and the perfectly understandable reluctance to face the painful realities make it all harder, but it is the ill-defined terrors that conjure up much worse horrors and strike dread into our hearts.

So we could try to begin talking to those around us about the stages or various aspects of dying, death and grief. These may be the most difficult conversations we will ever face, but it is surely worth attempting. There might well come times when all this is too much of a burden and we are too ill to cope with it, but we could mention the love and faith that will not let us go, whatever losses engulf us. Without trying to present ourselves as in some way saintly, it helps to be as specific as we can about exactly what does and does not frighten us and in what ways our beliefs equip us to confront what lies ahead. If we can get this out into the open, it cannot but help those near to us and us, too.

So, I have tried in a small way to reassure my family and best friends that I am not afraid of the process of dying, but am churned up by the prospect of leaving them. Often, widows and widowers feel they need some kind of permission to remarry, so, in an attempt to head off any false honouring of our memories, we can also encourage our families to enjoy life and meet new people after we have gone.

God, our loving Father, help me to face my death honestly,
and to comfort and prepare those who will be left behind.
Amen.

RACHEL BOULDING

St Brigid

To meet Brigid we need to go a long way back in time—to the fifth century, the early days of the Celtic church, which was the Christian presence in the north of England, Cornwall, Wales, Brittany, Scotland and Ireland. Those early days are hazy, with few written records; it is impossible to be certain exactly when Christianity arrived in Ireland, Brigid's home, though traditionally Patrick brought the faith in 432.

Brigid herself was born in the first half of the 450s, perhaps near Dundalk, County Louth. Her first written biography was produced in the seventh century and a second in the eighth. Recently, some scholars have claimed that Brigid did not exist at all and that the stories of her life are Christian versions of those told about the pagan goddess Brig, but most accept that she did exist, even if the stories we have are overlaid with legend.

The claimed connection with Brig is not surprising. Brigid lived at a time when paganism was still very much a living religion and Christianity was the newcomer. Brigid herself had a Christian mother and a pagan father. It was commonplace for the Christian missionaries to establish their churches and monasteries on or around pagan sacred sites, as a way of stressing the continuity of the new faith they offered with their hearers' existing faith. A holy woman such as Brigid would naturally have evoked comparisons with the holy women of the pagan faith and, in an oral culture, stories told of one might easily have become stories of the other.

A number of the elements that we see in the lives of the Celtic saints echo those of their pagan ancestors in faith. These include a deep respect for the environment, which led them to address God as 'Lord of the Elements'; a love of learning; a yearning to explore the unknown, perhaps inherited from the original Celtic peoples who wandered very widely; and the high value they placed on family and tribal belonging. To these, the early Christians added a love of silence and solitude, an appreciation of soul friendship and a joyful appreciation of ordinary life as the place of God's presence. Into this rich setting Brigid came and added her unique contribution.

HELEN JULIAN CSF

Fire of love

When the day of Pentecost had come, they were all together in one place. And suddenly from heaven there came a sound like the rush of a violent wind, and it filled the entire house where they were sitting. Divided tongues, as of fire, appeared among them, and a tongue rested on each of them. All of them were filled with the Holy Spirit and began to speak in other languages, as the Spirit gave them ability.

Fire is a common symbol in Christian spirituality, often representing the presence of the Holy Spirit, and it was a feature of Brigid's life from before she was born. Flame and a fiery pillar were seen rising from the house where her pregnant mother slept. After Brigid's birth, her mother went out to milk, leaving her alone in the house. Neighbours saw flames coming from the house and ran to rescue the child, but found her unharmed, and no fire burning.

Already we can see how God's presence, represented by fire, is both promise and danger. A story from later in Brigid's life is an example of her protective presence in relation to fire. When Brigid was receiving the veil as a nun, she bent down, holding a beam of the altar. The story is told that this beam was forever afterwards preserved from fire. The church in which it was burnt down three times, but this beam was always found undamaged among the ashes.

So it is not surprising that, at the monastery in Kildare that Brigid founded, the nuns were said to have kept a flame burning perpetually, a flame extinguished only at the time of the Reformation in the 16th century. The remains of the Fire House can still be seen near the present twelfth-century cathedral.

The Holy Spirit—God's presence with us—is both promise and danger. God's presence will both comfort and challenge, keeping us safe and burning away all that is not of God. The apostles were assured of the presence of the risen Jesus and were sent out to preach that message, which often brought them into danger, even death.

---

*Come Holy Spirit, fill the hearts of your faithful people
and kindle in them the fire of your love.*

HELEN JULIAN CSF

Child of a slave

The child grew, and was weaned; and Abraham made a great feast on the day that Isaac was weaned. But Sarah saw the son of Hagar the Egyptian, whom she had borne to Abraham, playing with her son Isaac. So she said to Abraham, 'Cast out this slave woman with her son; for the son of this slave woman shall not inherit along with my son Isaac.'… So Abraham rose early in the morning, and took bread and a skin of water, and gave it to Hagar, putting it on her shoulder, along with the child, and sent her away. And she departed, and wandered about in the wilderness of Beer-sheba.

Sometimes Bible stories, even very ancient ones, have contemporary resonance. This story of slavery, jealousy and a woman used and abused sadly finds echoes in the lives of trafficked women today. It is also the story of Brigid's mother.

Brigid's mother was a slave named Broicsech, bought by a man named Dubthach, a chieftain of Leinster. When Broicsech became pregnant by Dubthach, his wife was jealous and insisted that he must sell her or she would take her dowry and leave him. To his credit he was reluctant to do so, but eventually sold Broicsech to a poet, who in turn sold her to a druid. This may have been the same druid who had met Dubthach and Broicsech and prophesied that her child would be a wonderful radiant daughter, who would shine like the sun among the stars of heaven. He also prophesied that the children of Dubthach's wife would serve this child of a slave.

Slavery is taken for granted in the story of Brigid, as it is in the Bible. Paul may exhort masters to treat their slaves fairly (Ephesians 6:9), but even in the letter to Philemon about his escaped slave Onesimus, he only requests Philemon to treat the runaway as a 'beloved brother' (Philemon 16) and says nothing to suggest that slavery in itself is wrong.

This is one of the areas where our thinking has moved on.

What areas of slavery are you aware of today? Pray for those enslaved and consider how you might help to set them free.

HELEN JULIAN CSF

Threshold of faith

I am grateful to God—whom I worship with a clear conscience, as my ancestors did—when I remember you constantly in my prayers night and day. Recalling your tears, I long to see you so that I may be filled with joy. I am reminded of your sincere faith, a faith that lived first in your grandmother Lois and your mother Eunice and now, I am sure, lives in you. For this reason I remind you to rekindle the gift of God that is within you through the laying on of my hands; for God did not give us a spirit of cowardice, but rather a spirit of power and of love and of self-discipline.

Brigid had a mixed religious heritage. Her mother was a Christian, traditionally believed to have been baptised by Patrick, and her father a pagan. The druid who had bought her was obviously also pagan, but *his* uncle was a Christian.

This mixed heritage is well symbolised by the circumstances of Brigid's birth. Still working while heavily pregnant, at sunrise her mother was crossing the threshold of the house carrying a jug of milk when she gave birth. Two liminal moments came together—the sunrise, when darkness and night give way to day, and the threshold of the house, connecting the domestic with the wider world. Faith was at a similar place in Ireland in Brigid's time, with paganism and Christianity both present and widely accepted.

Stories from Brigid's early life show this. The druid seems to have accepted her Christian identity for, when she would not accept food from him, he believed it was because he was pagan and provided a cow to supply her with milk. Equally, when he heard her speaking in the night, he sent his Christian uncle to investigate and the uncle found her praying. There seems to have been respect and acceptance between the two faiths, alongside a desire on the part of the Christians to bring the pagans to their faith.

Later, when Brigid founded a monastery at Kildare, the church was built on the site of a pagan temple, 'baptising' it in God's service.

What is your religious heritage? Who are your 'mothers' in the faith?

HELEN JULIAN CSF

The gift of baptism

Then Jesus came from Galilee to John at the Jordan, to be baptised
by him. John would have prevented him, saying, 'I need to be baptised
by you, and do you come to me?' But Jesus answered him, 'Let it be
so now; for it is proper for us in this way to fulfil all righteousness.'
Then he consented. And when Jesus had been baptised, just as he
came up from the water, suddenly the heavens were opened to him
and he saw the Spirit of God descending like a dove and alighting on
him. And a voice from heaven said, 'This is my Son, the Beloved, with
whom I am well pleased.'

Whatever our heritage of faith, we still need to make our own
entrance into it and baptism is one of the key ways to do this. The
story of Brigid's baptism is unusual. According to her biographies, it
did not take place in a church, but was seen by the druid in a dream.
He saw three clerics in white hooded garments, who poured oil on
Brigid's head and baptised her, giving her the name Brigid. One of the
stories goes on to say that they were really three angels.

Whether by angels or clerics, Brigid was baptised as Jesus was and
given her name. The oil, still used in many baptisms today, is a sign
of anointing with the Holy Spirit, so it is a link to the stories of Brigid
and fire that we read a few days ago.

Many churches baptise new members as young children or babies,
so you may not remember your own baptism, as perhaps Brigid did
not remember hers. But it is important to reflect on it, to remember
that it has happened and that it has made a difference. Through baptism, we become beloved sons and daughters of God and begin a
lifelong journey of faith with our brothers and sisters in Christ—a
journey that God promises to share with us.

*God of grace, I thank you for the gift of baptism. Help me to remember
often my own baptism and give thanks that you have made me your
beloved daughter, your beloved son.*

HELEN JULIAN CSF

A very cheerful giver

The point is this: the one who sows sparingly will also reap sparingly, and the one who sows bountifully will also reap bountifully. Each of you must give as you have made up your mind, not reluctantly or under compulsion, for God loves a cheerful giver. And God is able to provide you with every blessing in abundance, so that by always having enough of everything, you may share abundantly in every good work. As it is written, 'He scatters abroad, he gives to the poor; his right-eousness endures for ever.' He who supplies seed to the sower and bread for food will supply and multiply your seed for sowing and increase the harvest of your righteousness.

Brigid must have been loved greatly by God, as her whole life was marked by cheerful giving. This generosity was not always welcomed by those around her. Later in her childhood she ended up living once again in her father Dubthach's household, but her stepmother demanded that he sell her once again, as she kept taking food and clothing to give to the poor.

Her father set out to see the king of Leinster and, while he was negotiating her sale, left her outside in the carriage. A leper came begging and Brigid gave him her father's sword—presumably the only item of value to hand. Not surprisingly, her father was livid when he discovered what she had done, but, when the king asked her why she had done this, her reply convinced him of her goodness and that she should neither be bought nor sold.

She encouraged others to generosity, too. A pair of stories tell of nuns who gave Brigid gifts of apples and sloes, which she promptly gave away to lepers. One of the nuns complained that she had given the gift to Brigid, not to lepers, while the other was happy to see the gift passed on. The trees of the first never bore fruit again, while those of the second bore two or three times their usual crop.

How easy do you find it to be generous? Do you worry that you may be left with not enough? How could you learn from today's passage and Brigid's example?

HELEN JULIAN CSF

A leading woman

I commend to you our sister Phoebe, a deacon of the church at Cenchreae, so that you may welcome her in the Lord as is fitting for the saints, and help her in whatever she may require from you, for she has been a benefactor of many and of myself as well. Greet Prisca and Aquila, who work with me in Christ Jesus, and who risked their necks for my life, to whom not only I give thanks, but also all the churches of the Gentiles... Greet Mary, who has worked very hard among you.

This passage from Romans is one of the key pieces of evidence for the role of women in leadership roles in the early church. The Celtic church in its practice drew from the society around it, which gave women similar legal rights to those of men and believed in their equality. Brigid, however, surpassed even what was normal in her church.

At the age of 14, her father decided to marry her off, but she refused and opted to become a nun. When, with her first sisters, she came to the bishop to 'take the veil', the ceremony which would make them officially nuns, Brigid hung back out of humility, but, perhaps recognising her leadership qualities, the bishop called her forward to be the first. Instead of reading the service for consecrating a nun over her, though, he found himself using the form for ordaining a bishop. His assistant protested, but the bishop replied that he did not have any power in this matter—it was God who had given her this status and dignity. As if in confirmation of this, a fiery pillar appeared over Brigid's head.

Whatever the truth of this story, the fact that it has survived means that some at least saw no problem if God had decided to make Brigid a bishop. Certainly she undertook tasks that would normally be priestly. For example, a story records her travelling to consecrate two new nuns and their house. Whatever the official rules, her leadership gifts were recognised and used.

God of all, thank you for the gifts you give to all your people.
Help us to use them well in your service.

HELEN JULIAN CSF

Religious pioneer

All who believed were together and had all things in common; they
would sell their possessions and goods and distribute the proceeds to
all, as any had need. Day by day, as they spent much time together in
the temple, they broke bread at home and ate their food with glad and
generous hearts, praising God and having the goodwill of all the people. And day by day the Lord added to their number those who were
being saved.

This passage from Acts is one of the foundational passages for religious life—the life of monks and nuns who live together and hold all
possessions in common. Brigid embraced this life at an early age and
continued in it until her death. She is credited with founding the
religious life for women in Ireland, at a point in time when it was still
very fluid, having no fixed form or rule. She founded communities
for both women and men at Kildare and ruled them both, along with
a bishop, Conleth, whom she selected for the task. The double monastery of women and men was a particular invention of the British
Isles. Hilda of Whitby was perhaps the most famous founder of such
a group, but at least another seven are known to have existed.

In the Celtic church, the life was influenced by the tribal society
in which it was set and was never confined only to vowed nuns and
monks. Monasteries had many lay people attached to them, who,
with their families, helped to grow crops and care for the animals.
The monks and nuns offered pastoral care and education and led the
worshipping life of the community.

Brigid's life was not confined to the monastery at Kildare: there are
many stories of her travelling throughout Ireland, visiting other holy
women and healing the sick. This pattern of communal life and outside ministry has been foundational for religious life, even if, for many
centuries, the outside ministry was forbidden for women. Indeed, the
Celtic pattern of communities made up of monks, nuns and lay people has been taken up by some new communities in recent decades.

Is the pattern of Acts reflected in your church life in any way?

HELEN JULIAN CSF

A miraculous cloak

Sing, O barren one who did not bear; burst into song and shout, you who have not been in labour! For the children of the desolate woman will be more than the children of her that is married, says the Lord. Enlarge the site of your tent, and let the curtains of your habitations be stretched out; do not hold back, lengthen your cords and strengthen your stakes. For you will spread out to the right and to the left, and your descendants will possess the nations and will settle the desolate towns.

One of my favourite stories about Brigid is how she obtained the land for a convent. She had found a perfect site, beside a forest, from which the sisters could obtain firewood and berries, and with a lake nearby for water. In addition, the land was fertile. It belonged to the king of Leinster, however, and, not surprisingly, when she asked for the land he just laughed at her and refused.

Brigid went away and prayed that God would soften the King's heart. Then she returned, smiled at the king and asked, 'Will you give me as much land as my cloak will cover?' The king, thinking she was joking, agreed. She gave her cloak to four of her sisters, who took a corner each. The king expected them to lay it flat on the ground, but, instead, they turned to face the four points of the compass and began to run, still holding the cloak. To the king's amazement, the cloak grew as they ran and soon it covered many acres of land.

He asked Brigid what was happening and she replied that her cloak would soon cover his whole province, to punish him for his stinginess. He begged her to call back her sisters and promised to give them the plot of land they wanted. Brigid agreed, but only had to mention the cloak after that, if the king was less than generous. He helped to build the convent, was always generous to the poor and, most important of all, became a Christian.

How could you be bolder in God's service?

HELEN JULIAN CSF

Healing and multiplication

After Jesus had left that place, he passed along the Sea of Galilee, and he went up the mountain, where he sat down. Great crowds came to him, bringing with them the lame, the maimed, the blind, the mute, and many others. They put them at his feet, and he cured them, so that the crowd was amazed when they saw the mute speaking, the maimed whole, the lame walking, and the blind seeing. And they praised the God of Israel.

In the stories of the saints we can often see the Gospel stories underlying them. Following Jesus was the main purpose of their lives, so doing what he did was a sign of their commitment and holiness.

Hence, there are many stories of Brigid healing the sick and multiplying food and drink. Even as a young girl, she had these gifts, ensuring there was always enough bread for her foster mother's guests, for example, and healing her with water drawn from a local well, which, after Brigid's prayer, was tasty and intoxicating.

In her father's house, she was given a piece of bacon to boil for a guest, but a hungry dog appeared, so she gave him first one fifth, then another fifth. When her father returned, however, he found the whole piece of bacon intact. This is an example of her care for those in need, both people and animals.

She also multiplied butter and produced large amounts of ale from a single sack of malt (a nice example of 'translating' a Gospel miracle, that of Jesus turning water into wine, for the local context). She healed many lepers, including one who had to be persuaded that it was better to be healed than remain leprous, which provided good opportunities for begging.

Brigid even stilled a storm. She was visiting another nun and had gone out to pasture her sheep in terrible weather—rain and wind, thunder and lightning. Brigid sang a song and the storm was stilled.

As Christians, we are all called to follow in Jesus' footsteps, but we often find it challenging to do as he did. How might Brigid's example encourage you to make one small step in faith?

HELEN JULIAN CSF

Preaching the gospel

Then [the jailer] brought [Paul and Silas] outside and said, 'Sirs, what must I do to be saved?' They answered, 'Believe on the Lord Jesus, and you will be saved, you and your household.' They spoke the word of the Lord to him and to all who were in his house. At the same hour of the night he took them and washed their wounds; then he and his entire family were baptised without delay. He brought them up into the house and set food before them; and he and his entire family rejoiced that he had become a believer in God.

As we have seen in the story of the king of Leinster, encounters with Brigid often led to conversion to Christ. She used whatever opportunities came to hand. One of the most famous of these is the origin of Brigid's cross—traditionally made and blessed on her feast day.

The story goes that she was nursing a pagan chieftain who was close to death. In some versions of the story, this man is her own father. As she sat praying by his bedside, she wove a cross from the rushes on the floor. He asked about its meaning and was so overwhelmed by what she told him that he was baptised before his death.

Another opportunity came when a householder, having seen Brigid perform a miracle, asked her to come and bless his house. When she came, however, she refused to do so or even to eat with him because she knew that no one in the house had been baptised, except the slave who had been sent to fetch her. When the householder heard this, he agreed to be baptised and Brigid sent for a priest. Then she both accepted his hospitality and blessed his house. After this she always had a priest as her charioteer, so as to be able to offer baptism to anyone she met.

The stories of conversion are told in a very matter of fact way; they are simply part of what Brigid does as she travels around. She seems always to have been open to the opportunities before her.

Loving God, may I be willing to seize the opportunities you give
me to preach your gospel.

HELEN JULIAN CSF

Trinity of saints

Now there are varieties of gifts, but the same Spirit; and there are varieties of services, but the same Lord; and there are varieties of activities, but it is the same God who activates all of them in everyone. To each is given the manifestation of the Spirit for the common good... For just as the body is one and has many members, and all the members of the body, though many, are one body, so it is with Christ. For in the one Spirit we were all baptised into one body—Jews or Greeks, slaves or free—and we were all made to drink of one Spirit.

Ireland has a 'holy trinity' of early saints. Brigid is one and the other two are Patrick and Columcille, also known as Columba. Brigid and Patrick shared the experience of slavery—Brigid from birth, Patrick in his teens and early 20s, when he was captured from his home on the west coast of Britain and taken to Ireland. After escaping, he trained for the priesthood and experienced the monastic life in Gaul, before returning to Ireland as a missionary bishop. Columcille travelled in the other direction. After ordination he founded monasteries in Ireland and had a ministry of preaching and teaching before leaving to live on Iona. So, all three shared a commitment to the monastic life and evangelism.

There are stories of friendship between Brigid and Patrick, of her setting out to visit him and ask for his blessing. Their shared love for Ireland and its people and desire to see them come to Christ made for a strong bond between them.

This 'trinity' is a demonstration of the different ways in which the Spirit works within the church. Each of these saints seems to have had a clear sense of the work to which God was calling them, whether it was Patrick returning to Ireland, Columcille leaving his home country to be an evangelist among the Picts or Brigid founding the monastic life for women and working for its growth. Their different gifts and life experiences were all used in God's service.

What gift have you been given and what service are you called to?

HELEN JULIAN CSF

God's eternal now

[Jesus said] 'Very truly, I tell you, whoever keeps my word will never see death.' The Jews said to him, 'Now we know that you have a demon. Abraham died, and so did the prophets; yet you say, "Whoever keeps my word will never taste death." Are you greater than our father Abraham, who died?'... Jesus answered... 'Your ancestor Abraham rejoiced that he would see my day; he saw it and was glad.' Then the Jews said to him, 'You are not yet fifty years old, and have you seen Abraham?' Jesus said to them, 'Very truly, I tell you, before Abraham was, I am.'

The stories of Brigid and Patrick meeting illustrate a fascinating aspect of the Celtic view of life. The reality is that if we accept the usual dates for their lives, Brigid would have been a young child when Patrick died, so it is unlikely that they met. Certainly the meetings recorded in Brigid's biographies cannot have happened.

So what is going on? Why are these stories told? There are probably two things at work here. One is a desire to show Brigid as the equal of the great Patrick. If they met and he accepted her ministry alongside his own, this would be an endorsement of her standing.

The more interesting thing is the Celts' understanding of time. They saw time as a gift from God, a sacred reality that had already been blessed by God, so all of time—past, present and future—is always present now. Thus, linear time, with one event following another, did not limit the early Celts. It therefore made perfect sense to them for those who shared the same qualities and holiness, such as Patrick and Brigid, to have been friends, in God's eternal now.

This understanding of time also explains what might seem the bizarre story that Brigid, along with Ita, were midwives to Mary, helping to bring Jesus to birth. In some accounts, Brigid was looking after the inn in Bethlehem when Mary and Joseph arrived. In God's time there is only the present.

God of all time, help me to live in the security of your present moment.

HELEN JULIAN CSF

Gifts of wisdom

At Gibeon the Lord appeared to Solomon in a dream by night; and God said, 'Ask what I should give you.'... And Solomon said... 'Give your servant therefore an understanding mind to govern your people, able to discern between good and evil; for who can govern this your great people?' It pleased the Lord that Solomon had asked this. God said to him,'... I now do according to your word. Indeed I give you a wise and discerning mind; no one like you has been before you and no one like you shall arise after you.'

Immediately after this passage, Solomon is faced with two women, both claiming to be the mother of the same child, and gives his famous judgement, showing his wisdom. Brigid, too, had gifts of wisdom and discernment. We have seen, for example, how she knew that a household to which she had been invited was pagan. One of her visits to Patrick also included a judgement like that of Solomon.

When she arrived, a group of members of the clergy were trying to settle a paternity dispute. A woman claimed that the father of her newborn son was Bron, one of their bishops, but he denied the charge. When Brigid arrived, they asked her to arbitrate. She asked the woman, who repeated her claim, but Brigid did not believe her and she asked the child directly. Although he was too young to speak, he did speak and identified his father as 'a certain low and ill-shaped man' and not the bishop in question at all. Brigid had compassion on the woman and saved her from being burnt for lying, requiring only that she did penance.

Stories in biographies of saints (hagiographies) often echo those of the Bible, especially, but not only, the stories about Jesus. The hearers and readers were meant to be aware of the parallels and be inspired to follow Jesus' example, as the saint had done. The truth of the stories operates at a level deeper than simply the factual, revealing the deeper motivations and gifts of the saint.

Gracious God, give me the gifts I need to serve you and
courage to use them.

HELEN JULIAN CSF

Rekindling the flame

The Lord will guide you continually, and satisfy your needs in parched places, and make your bones strong; and you shall be like a watered garden, like a spring of water, whose waters never fail. Your ancient ruins shall be rebuilt; you shall raise up the foundations of many generations; you shall be called the repairer of the breach, the restorer of streets to live in.

The story comes full circle. Although very little remains of Brigid's monastery in Kildare almost 1500 years after her death, her life continues to inspire people today. The Anglican St Brigid's Cathedral stands on the site of her monastery and just a short distance away is St Brigid's Roman Catholic church, built originally in 1833 and rebuilt in 1975. The altar is in the shape of Brigid's cross.

Women have also chosen to follow her once again in monastic life. Her community in Kildare came to an end at the time of the Reformation and the sacred flame was extinguished, but, in 1807, the Sisters of St Brigid were refounded in Ireland and spread throughout many parts of the world, including Australia, New Zealand, Papua New Guinea and Mexico—countries Brigid could not have imagined. In 1992, a small group came to live in Kildare, where they care for pilgrims and seek to make the spirit of Brigid available to all.

In 1993 the sisters relit the sacred flame at the opening of a justice and peace conference celebrating Brigid's legacy. They continue to tend the flame at Solas Bhride, their Christian Centre for Celtic Spirituality, which has recently opened new buildings to house the increasing numbers of pilgrims. In 2005, the local council commissioned a sculpture to be placed in Kildare town square to house the flame. The flame, taken from that at the sisters' centre, was lit on 1 February 2006 by the then President of the Irish Republic.

Look back over the notes on Brigid. How might you be inspired by some aspect of her life? Are there parts of your life that are parched, which her life and example might water and bring back to life? Is there some 'rebuilding' to which she is calling you?

HELEN JULIAN CSF

Paul's letter to the Ephesians

'Is there a letter in the bag for me?' asked the Beatles.

Every time I see the postie approaching, I rush to the door. There is nothing quite like getting a letter! Not an email or a text, but a proper letter, handwritten, full of personality. All that time, care, even love put down on paper. Not many come through the letterbox these days.

In our loft there is a box with all the letters we wrote—every day—when we were going out, but were apart… ahhh! The last time we took the box down and read this ancient archive, we were surprised to discover so many apologies for the last phone call—of being abrupt, failing to understand, feeling tired, stressed—but of course there is no record of the phone calls themselves, so it is not always clear what prompted the precise wording of the letter.

We have no idea what prompted Paul to write to the young congregation in Ephesus. When the letter arrived (probably between AD60 and 62), however, like ours, it was part of an ongoing conversation. It began when Paul briefly visited Ephesus on his second Mediterranean tour (Acts 18:19–21). Then he returned and stayed for about three years (AD52–55). Acts 19 reveals it was an eventful time. He introduced the believers to the Holy Spirit. Every day he went to the meeting hall to speak about Jesus. He performed miracles. He broke the power of witchcraft, put idol makers out of work, caused a riot… then it was time to move on!

So, they knew Paul well, but they never saw him again. They would have heard of his arrest, that he was being sent to Rome. They almost certainly had other letters from him and, almost certainly, would have had letters and news from them.

When this letter arrived, they would have been excited, full of expectation, keen to know what the apostle had to say to them.

How about you? For the next 14 days, this is God's letter to you. Are you excited? Full of expectation? Keen to know what he has to say to you? By God's Spirit, this letter can be as fresh to you as it was to the Ephesians—part of God's ongoing conversation with you.

STEPHEN RAND

'Let's start at the very beginning...'

Paul, an apostle of Christ Jesus by the will of God, To God's holy people in Ephesus, the faithful in Christ Jesus: Grace and peace to you
from God our Father and the Lord Jesus Christ. Praise be to the God
and Father of our Lord Jesus Christ, who has blessed us in the heavenly realms with every spiritual blessing in Christ.

We sign our name at the end of a letter. In Paul's day, you put your
name right at the start, so, straight away, the reader knew who was
writing. Then Paul immediately identifies himself—and at the same
time establishes his authority, the reason his letter carries weight. He
is an 'apostle'—someone sent on a mission, an ambassador. This is
not a job or a church appointment; he represents Jesus, he works for
Jesus, he is appointed by God.

He is writing to 'God's holy people' (v. 1) in this wording, but
older versions of the Bible say 'saints'. The New Testament regards all
faithful followers of Jesus as saints. That means it is possible for you
to stand in front of a mirror and see a saint!

Now we get to the greeting: 'Grace and peace' (v. 2). These two
words appear many more times in this letter. They are more than a
greeting, they are the announcement of a vital theme. The Greeks
usually began with 'greetings', but the Greek words for 'greetings'
and 'grace' are very similar—Paul is almost using a pun.

'Peace' was the Hebrew greeting—'shalom'. It carried a hint of
everything that God intended when he set people at the heart of his
creation: wholeness, well-being, right and rewarding relationships
with God, with each other, with everything God had made.

So 'grace and peace' is a greeting that brings Greeks and Jews
together, just as God, in his grace, had made a new creation in the
church, which was also about bringing Greeks and Jews together to
experience and share in the peace of God. No wonder the first line
of this letter is a shout of praise to God for all his blessings!

*Is there someone you could write a letter to bring encouragement
and give them a reason to praise God for his grace and peace?*

STEPHEN RAND

Chosen, adopted, redeemed, forgiven...

For he chose us in him before the creation of the world to be holy and blameless in his sight. In love he predestined us for adoption for sonship through Jesus Christ, in accordance with his pleasure and will—to the praise of his glorious grace, which he has freely given us in the One he loves. In him we have redemption through his blood, the forgiveness of sins, in accordance with the riches of God's grace that he lavished on us with all wisdom and understanding.

In the original Greek, verses 3–14 are one long sentence—a rolling, joyous hymn of praise for all that God has done for us.

Chosen: God loves me so much that he took the initiative to reach out to me. Not because I am better than anyone else, not because I am deserving; simply because of his love. It is a wonderful privilege. It is also a great challenge and responsibility, because I have been chosen for a purpose—to be holy and blameless, set aside for God and by God to live in the right way.

Adopted: I am more than a follower, I have been brought in to the heart of God's royal family. Because the Son of God loved me and died for me, I too can become a son of God, one of his children, with all the blessings, rights and privileges that go with being one of the family. This gender-specific language jars a little in the 21st century, but, in Paul's day, it was the son who inherited from the father. So, Paul is emphasising that, whether male or female, we can all inherit the full blessings coming from the Father.

Redeemed: another legal illustration. The slave is set free for ever because the price has been paid in full.

Forgiven: not just a child of God, fully liberated. The barriers have gone, the slate wiped clean; there is no more guilt and no more punishment in view.

These are the riches of God's grace, lavished on us. This is a hymn worth singing!

Gracious Father, thank you for all you have done and are doing and will do—for me.

STEPHEN RAND

Keep asking

For this reason, ever since I heard about your faith in the Lord Jesus and your love for all God's people, I have not stopped giving thanks for you, remembering you in my prayers. I keep asking that the God of our Lord Jesus Christ, the glorious Father, may give you the Spirit of wisdom and revelation, so that you may know him better. I pray that the eyes of your heart may be enlightened in order that you may know the hope to which he has called you, the riches of his glorious inheritance in his holy people, and his incomparably great power for us who believe.

Imagine being in Ephesus and reading this letter. Would your heart not burst with the affirmation, the encouragement and positivity of Paul's words? It is great when people say good things about you, especially when it is on the basis of your reputation, on what they have been hearing about you.

Then, on top of all these words of praise, Paul tells you that he cannot stop thanking God for you and praying for you!

There are few greater privileges in life than having faithful people pray for you. I grew up in a small church that was like an extended family. I am now 65. There is one precious lady—still 'Aunty' to me—who babysat me when I was tiny—and still prays for me each and every day. There were others who did the same, but I think she is the last one still with us. She will be 90 this month. Even as I write this, there is a tear of gratitude in my eye.

Savour the words of Paul's prayer. Imagine them being prayed over you. He longed for the Ephesians to be so close to Christ, in such an intimate relationship that they would know him better—and from that would come hope, spiritual riches and great power—everything Jesus offers realised in our lives.

Read today's passage out loud—except, every time it says 'you' or 'your', insert your own name. Do it again, this time inserting the names of those you care about most. Finally, remembering my 'Aunty', keep doing it for her and others!

STEPHEN RAND

Dead... alive... raised

As for you, you were dead in your transgressions and sins, in which you used to live when you followed the ways of this world... Like the rest, we were by nature deserving of wrath. But because of his great love for us, God, who is rich in mercy, made us alive with Christ even when we were dead in transgressions—it is by grace you have been saved. And God raised us up with Christ and seated us with him in the heavenly realms in Christ Jesus.

Paul's theology is stark... and glorious! This is a wonderful summary of why the gospel of Jesus is such good news.

He starts with the underlying spiritual reality of the whole human race: we are dead. Physically living, but spiritually dead. The Ephesians are described as those who 'followed the ways of this world' (v. 2). This is a deliberate contrast with the phrase first used to describe Christians: followers of 'the Way' (Acts 9:2). It is a reminder of the words of Jesus in the Sermon on the Mount: 'But small is the gate and narrow the road that leads to life' (Matthew 7:14).

Jesus also said that the broad road, the easy way, led to destruction. Paul writes that this is what we deserve. Then, however, there is a 'but'—and a big 'but'! We do not get what we deserve (which is a simple but profound definition of grace). Why not? Because of God's 'great love' and 'rich... mercy' (Ephesians 2:4). He took the initiative. Just as he first breathed life into humankind (Genesis 2:7), he has now 'made us alive' (Ephesians 2:5). This is the greatest act of CPR in history!

Even this is not the whole story. We are raised with Christ and seated with him. The new life is one of both intimacy and grandeur. We are sitting with Jesus, on the throne where he is king of kings. Notice how often the word 'with' is used: we are made 'alive with Christ' (v. 5), 'raised... with Christ', 'seated... with him' (v. 6). When we follow Jesus, we walk with him, we share in his experience of new life, resurrection, glory.

This is the good news of what Jesus has done—the living dead are made the dead who live!

STEPHEN RAND

The gift of God

> For it is by grace you have been saved, through faith—and this is not
> from yourselves, it is the gift of God—not by works, so that no one
> can boast. For we are God's handiwork, created in Christ Jesus to do
> good works, which God prepared in advance for us to do.

So many, inside and outside the church, are convinced that if we do
our best, then we will get to heaven. Two thousand years ago, Paul
was absolutely clear: new life is a gift. There is nothing we can do to
earn it and we certainly do not deserve it.

Then there are also so many, inside and outside the church, who
believe that we do not have to do anything. God loves us all, so he
will be ready and willing to share eternal life with everyone, regardless of their behaviour or even their wishes. Two thousand years ago,
Paul was absolutely clear: to receive God's gracious gift we have to
respond with faith.

The bus has arrived. Its destination is clearly marked on the front.
We can believe the bus can take us there, but we will not get there
unless we take the step of faith—and get on the bus.

Some people want to work hard to get to God—they do not
receive the gift. Some people do not work hard to share God's love
with others—they waste, even abuse, the gift.

Salvation, God's gift of life, is not just about the drowning man
being dragged to the shore and given the kiss of life. It is about being
set on your feet, walking in a new direction, given a purpose in life,
living life as God intended.

Christians should do good. As an old friend used to say, 'You can't
become a dog by barking, but you can tell a dog by its bark.'

---

*The gift is there, right in front of us. It is not even wrapped
up—we can clearly see what it is: life, salvation. We just have
to open our arms and open our hearts to receive it. Then we
can enjoy it, revel in it. I love watching my grandchildren on
Christmas Day—they know what to do with gifts!*

STEPHEN RAND

One new humanity

Remember that at that time you were separate from Christ, excluded from citizenship in Israel and foreigners to the covenants of the promise, without hope and without God in the world. But now in Christ Jesus you who once were far away have been brought near by the blood of Christ. For he himself is our peace, who has made the two groups one and has destroyed the barrier, the dividing wall of hostility... His purpose was to create in himself one new humanity out of the two, thus making peace.

Paul has already described what Jesus does as making dead people alive. Now he looks at this from another angle. It is as if the precious stone is turned so that a different facet can sparkle in the light.

He addresses a new dimension of the human condition. Before Jesus came, the Jews had a revelation of God and access to him. They had been chosen to receive God's promises of blessing—the 'covenants'. None of this was available to the Gentiles, the non-Jews. They were 'foreigners', excluded, alienated, 'without hope and without God'. When Jesus died, however, the temple curtain that sealed off the Holy of Holies was torn open—the barrier to the presence of God was seen to be removed. Now the Gentiles, who had been so far away, were 'brought near' into God's presence. Their alienation was ended.

Not only was the barrier to God removed, so they could enjoy a new relationship with him, but also the 'dividing wall' (as there was, literally, in the temple) between Jew and Gentile was removed. They, too, could enjoy a new relationship, made possible by Jesus' death.

He is the ultimate peacemaker. Indeed, he is peace personified, because when an individual is united with him, that person is also united with all the others who share in his life. The church is the fulfilment of God's purpose to create 'one new humanity', to demonstrate to the world how ethnic, cultural and spiritual barriers can be broken down and positive peace can be lived, cherished and shared.

Make me, my church and the church worldwide a channel
of your peace.

STEPHEN RAND

God lives here

You are no longer foreigners and strangers, but fellow citizens with God's people and also members of his household, built on the foundation of the apostles and prophets, with Christ Jesus himself as the chief cornerstone. In him the whole building is joined together and rises to become a holy temple in the Lord. And in him you too are being built together to become a dwelling in which God lives by his Spirit.

The precious stone is turned again; new facets gleam and sparkle. The metaphors tumble from Paul's pen, almost too fast to take in.

Before Jesus died and rose again to create one new humanity, non-Jews were either foreigners (people living outside the boundaries and benefits of God's people) or strangers (those who lived within the borders, but had no rights as citizens; they were passing through, with no rights of residency—rather like 'asylum seekers' today). Now, though, Jews and non-Jews have become 'fellow citizens' (v. 19). They have equal standing, sharing the same rights, privileges and responsibilities. They have also become family, 'members of his household' (v. 19), so they share the same relationship. In a few words Paul conveys a unity rooted in objective reality and emotional warmth.

From the household, Paul's thoughts jump to the house, the building, and another picture is introduced. The church is a spiritual building. Its foundation is the apostles and prophets—those who bring God's unchanging message and those who interpret it in relation to each specific situation. Jesus is the 'chief cornerstone' (v. 20)—the one on whom the whole structure rests, with each stone or brick lined up in accordance with his guidance. Alternatively, this could be translated as 'keystone'—the one on whom all others depend.

Christ is also the builder. He is building everyone together, creating a place where God will live by his Spirit. Tomorrow you may be with your fellow churchgoers, all together in a building, worshipping God, but God is not waiting to meet you in that building. Rather, individually and corporately, he is living in you and through you.

Keep building your church, dear Father, and keep building me into it.

STEPHEN RAND

Filled with love, filled with God's fullness

I pray that out of his glorious riches he may strengthen you with power through his Spirit in your inner being, so that Christ may dwell in your hearts through faith. And I pray that you, being rooted and established in love, may have power, together with all the Lord's holy people, to grasp how wide and long and high and deep is the love of Christ, and to know this love that surpasses knowledge—that you may be filled to the measure of all the fullness of God.

This prayer is beautiful, complex, moving and profound. It overflows with adjectives trying to encompass realities almost indescribable.

Love is at its heart. Our lives are 'rooted and established' (v. 17) in God's love. It is the source of all our nourishment; it gives stability and growth. By God's power, coming from his glorious riches, we can know this unknowable love—and not just know about it but also know it by experience, filled to overflowing. What a prayer; what a possibility!

I have grasped this prayer gratefully for myself, but it was written for a church. I need to know God's love personally, individually, but I can know it even more as part of a group of God's people. Never give up on finding others who can offer mutual encouragement and inspiration to be filled with God's love.

There is more: the phrase 'together with all the Lord's holy people' (v. 18). Paul wanted them to think of the whole worldwide Church. I have grasped so much of the extent of God's love from my involvement with Christians facing extreme poverty and awful persecution that I think they have given me some insight into the fullness of God.

Pray this prayer for yourself and then for the people you care about most. I will pledge to pray it today as well, for you and every reader of these notes. May Christ dwell in your heart through faith. 'Now to him who is able to do immeasurably more than all we ask or imagine, according to his power that is at work within us, to him be glory in the church and in Christ Jesus throughout all generations, for ever and ever! Amen' (Ephesians 3:20–21).

STEPHEN RAND

One for all, all for oneness

As a prisoner for the Lord, then, I urge you to live a life worthy of the calling you have received. Be completely humble and gentle; be patient, bearing with one another in love. Make every effort to keep the unity of the Spirit through the bond of peace. There is one body and one Spirit, just as you were called to one hope when you were called; one Lord, one faith, one baptism; one God and Father of all, who is over all and through all and in all.

Chapters 1—3 are full of teaching about what Christ has done—'to him be glory in the church' (3:21)—while emphasising that the purpose of Christ's death is to transform our lives and behaviour. Now Paul indicates how this glory should be expressed in our daily life.

Christians are 'called', people with a vocation, and he urges them to live accordingly. The Greek literally means 'walk worthily'. It is as if Jesus has gone ahead and calls us to follow; we are to walk towards him, step by step, in a straight line.

He sees maintaining unity—'make every effort' (4:3)—as a vital part of this process. The four virtues he urges on us (humility, gentleness, patience and forbearance) are those that perhaps contribute most to unity among a group of Christians!

'Bearing with one another' (v. 2): what a challenge?! People in my church can be so irritating! Also, you have to bear with them 'in love', doing the best for them, building them up, not putting them down. Paul knew it was demanding; he knew it would be an effort. That is why he underlines the reason: Jesus died to break down barriers and bring unity. Oneness is at the core of the kingdom; there is a 'bond of peace' (v. 3) that holds it all together.

Here, every resident moving on to the new estate nearby is welcomed with a card and a cake on behalf of all the churches in Bicester. Some specifically comment that it is good to see churches working together. Unity is a witness to the reality of Jesus.

'Bind us together, Lord, with cords that cannot be broken.'

STEPHEN RAND

Equipping, building, maturing

Christ himself gave the apostles, the prophets, the evangelists, the pastors and teachers, to equip his people for works of service, so that the body of Christ may be built up until we all reach unity in the faith and in the knowledge of the Son of God and become mature, attaining to the whole measure of the fullness of Christ… From him the whole body, joined and held together by every supporting ligament, grows and builds itself up in love.

Five gifts from Christ to his church; five roles that enable a church to function as God intends, to be built up and mature.

There are missionary-messengers, providing a foundation in the truth; there are those who speak God's word into the specific situation of the church; there are gifted individuals who can explain the gospel and encourage people to follow Jesus; there are those who care for the flock and those who feed the flock. These are not jobs to be filled, but responsibilities to be fulfilled.

A church may pay someone to carry out some of these tasks. What matters is that all of these gifts are being received and applied within the church. More than that, they are to be shared and multiplied. Each of these functions is to 'equip his people for works of service' (v. 12). That is how the church is built up and matures, with everyone playing their part. There is more to church than the pastor and teacher, focused on a Sunday service.

Paul's vision of the church here includes those who are focused on sharing the good news of Jesus and all the functions are intended to equip the congregation to serve—inside and outside the church.

It is vital that churches engage with and serve their local communities, both as a church body and as individual church members live and work in their communities. A mature church is a missional church!

Do I know what gift I have to bring to the life of my church, in the church and in the community? Do I know what part I am called to play to equip and build up others? Am I playing my part?

STEPHEN RAND

Your new self

You were taught, with regard to your former way of life, to put off your old self, which is being corrupted by its deceitful desires; to be made new in the attitude of your minds; and to put on the new self, created to be like God in true righteousness and holiness.

When Paul wrote this letter, people deciding to follow Christ were baptised, which still happens in many churches today. These verses resemble Paul's words in Romans 6:4—'We were therefore buried with him through baptism into death in order that, just as Christ was raised from the dead… we too may live a new life'—so it is possible they come from a specific set of teachings, a catechism, for those preparing for baptism.

They certainly reinforce a key point for Paul, that doctrinal truth must be reflected in everyday behaviour. This time the analogy is that just as you change your clothes, so you take off your old self and put on your new self. It is a limited analogy as we change our clothes all the time, but this is, generally, a once and for all act. 'Anyone who belongs to Christ has become a new person. The old life is gone; a new life has begun!' (2 Corinthians 5:17, NLT). Two words for 'new' are used in the original text. One is translated 'made new' or 'renewed'. This emphasises that I am the same person, but transformed, revitalised, given a whole new lease of life. This renewal happens in our minds and affects our attitudes, which in turn govern our behaviour.

I recently visited Olney, where John Newton was a curate. He was a slave trader and became a Christian, but did not immediately become an abolitionist. Eventually he rejected slavery completely and backed Wilberforce. Over time his mind and attitudes were renewed.

The other word for 'new' means a new start, a new creation. Human beings were created in the image of God (Genesis 1:27). A Christian is recreated in the image of God so that he or she can live life as God intended.

The new creation is both a fact and a process:
we must become what we are.

STEPHEN RAND

Filled with the Spirit

Live a life of love, just as Christ loved us and gave himself up for us as a fragrant offering and sacrifice to God... Be very careful, then, how you live... do not be foolish, but understand what the Lord's will is. Do not get drunk on wine, which leads to debauchery. Instead, be filled with the Spirit... Sing and make music from your heart to the Lord, always giving thanks to God the Father for everything.

Paul summarises God's guide to right behaviour: 'live a life of love' (v. 2). I should write this on the inside and outside of my front door, so I read it every time I leave the house... and every time I return! In public and in private, I must live a life of love.

This is the wise way to live. It is foolish to ignore God's will. I think this is more than an instruction; it is an observation. There are millions whose lives—and those of many others—are wrecked and ruined by their own bad behaviour; many of them wish they had made wiser decisions.

When I was first at university, I got so drunk one evening that I was ill all night. I learned my lesson! Many do not and alcohol excess is identified as a major cause of crime, accidents and family break-down in our society. God's way to live is the wise way to live.

The only way we can live wisely is to feel the presence of God's Spirit in our lives. Filled with his Spirit, our thoughts and actions are constantly guided by him. One way that will show is in our worship. When our lives are full of God we will enjoy gathering with others to sing his praises.

The second indication of the Spirit-filled life is thankfulness. We can give thanks for everything when we know that nothing can separate us from the love of God.

There are many styles of worship. All can be full of the life of God or all can be deathly. It is the presence of the Spirit of God in the worshippers that brings worship to life and enables us to live a life of love.

STEPHEN RAND

Submission and love

Submit to one another out of reverence for Christ. Wives, submit yourselves to your own husbands as you do to the Lord. For the husband is the head of the wife as Christ is the head of the church, his body, of which he is the Saviour… Husbands, love your wives, just as Christ loved the church and gave himself up for her… In this same way, husbands ought to love their wives as their own bodies. He who loves his wife loves himself.

Here is an important fact: if you have headings in your Bible, they are not part of the original text! Many editions rightly include 'submit to one another' with the previous section, because it is quite possible that Paul intended this mutual submission to be another outworking of being filled with the Spirit. Then a heading appears something like 'Instructions to wives and husbands'. When the Bible reading part of the wedding service is reached and the passage starts, 'Wives, submit yourselves to your own husbands…' (v. 22), the husbands present look smug and the wives roll their eyes.

I love to preach from this passage at a wedding. It reveals a radical blueprint for equality in marriage, not a justification for male oppression. Sadly, there is evidence that women suffer as much domestic violence in Christian marriages as in wider society—possibly more. The church needs to speak up to end this tragic epidemic.

These verses are not a recipe for decision making. They are a specific outworking of the Ephesians theme of unity. Unity in marriage stems from the mutual submission demanded of all Christians: 'Do nothing out of selfish ambition or vain conceit, but in humility value others above yourselves' (Philippians 2:3). It is in this context that wives are to submit to their husbands. Equally, husbands are to love their wives as Christ loved the church—sacrificially, completely—the highest possible standard of love. Christian marriages should reveal the nature of God's love to a watching world.

Christ is the head of the church. He brought it into being, he loves it, he died for it, he is devoted to it still. That is who we are called to follow.

STEPHEN RAND

Stand firm

Finally, be strong in the Lord… Put on the full armour of God, so that you can take your stand against the devil's schemes. For our struggle is not against flesh and blood, but against the rulers, against the authorities, against the powers of this dark world and against the spiritual forces of evil in the heavenly realms… Stand firm then, with the belt of truth… the breastplate of righteousness… your feet fitted with the readiness that comes from the gospel of peace… Take up the shield of faith… the helmet of salvation and the sword of the Spirit, which is the word of God.

Ephesians is packed with sublime expressions of wonderful grace, lavish love and great glory, but it ends with gritty reality: we are in a battle. Paul was in prison. Every day he would see the soldiers, symbols of the power of the greatest empire the world had seen, but they were not the ultimate enemy. The real battle was against the spiritual forces of evil—a far greater power than the Roman Empire.

Becoming a Christian is not opting for the sunlounger by the pool in the rose garden, but the front line of a spiritual battle. The enemy's first tactic is to do everything possible to hide this from us and we prefer a cosy gospel to a costly gospel, so we can be taken in. Yet the media ceaselessly provides us with the evidence of the battle. It may be spiritual, but it has very real and devastating casualties. Global conflict fuelled by greed, cruel ideologies that crush compassion, family breakdown, addictions and abuse.

So Paul looks at his guards and analyses how they are prepared to fight. They take their stand, ready to defend themselves, so he urges us to focus on truth, determined to do the right thing (righteousness), with the faith to believe that God, the victor, is with us whatever the situation and has guaranteed our safety and ultimate salvation. We can fight back—the Spirit of God revealed in the word of God is the ultimate weapon.

Father, help me to recognise the battle and see you win significant victories in me and through me, by your Spirit.

STEPHEN RAND

The character of David

Just over a thousand years before the birth of Jesus, his ancestor, David, was anointed by the prophet Samuel as the successor to Saul, the first king of Israel. The early heady days of Saul's kingship had turned sour and Samuel received a disturbing word from the Lord that God was aggrieved he had made Saul king, for he had turned from God's ways (1 Samuel 15:11). Thus, Samuel's new duty was to nurture the king-in-waiting.

In the 15 years between the anointing and the start of his rule as king, David lived in a dangerous world of the increasingly unstable King Saul. During these years, however, many of David's qualities came to light and they proved to be ones that made him a remarkable and inspiring king and leader, such that even today millions of people across the globe thumb through the stories of this shepherd king and draw inspiration from his example. Furthermore, David was a prolific songwriter, with 73 of the 150 Psalms being attributed to him. Even if there are scholars who speculate about his authorship of some of these, few could deny that what we find in these beautiful psalms are themes, longings, explorations and insights consistent with the character of David portrayed in the books of Samuel, Kings and Chronicles.

In the coming two weeks, we shall study some of the qualities of David. He would be the first to tell us that he was not without his flaws, but he is undoubtedly one of the most intriguing and inspiring characters of the Bible. It is not surprising that when, a millennium later, Jesus entered Jerusalem on the back of a donkey, the crowds chose to hail him as the 'Son of David'. I suspect it was more than a celebration of the family connection and more than the making of a theological point. The people recognised something in Jesus—qualities in this humble yet powerful king that harked back to the heyday of King David. It would surely be David's desire that, as we read again his stories, we would be drawn in our hearts and minds to the King of kings.

MICHAEL MITTON

The faith-fuelled courage

The Philistine said to David, 'Come to me, and I will give your flesh to
the birds of the air and to the wild animals of the field.' But David said
to the Philistine, 'You come to me with sword and spear and javelin;
but I come to you in the name of the Lord of hosts, the God of the
armies of Israel, whom you have defied. This very day the Lord will
deliver you into my hand.'

We start this series of notes on David with one of the most famous
stories of the Bible: that of David and Goliath. David is the youngest
of Jesse's sons. God, who looks not at the outer appearance but into
the heart (1 Samuel 16:7), has seen qualities in David and tells Samuel
to anoint him as the future king. The Philistines are a powerful force,
always threatening the Israelites and they currently sport a nine-foot
giant called Goliath, who clearly unnerves the Israelites (1 Samuel
17:11). Jesse has three sons in the army and sends David with supplies for his brothers, but, on arrival, David is stirred with indignation
at the threats of the Philistines and offers to take on Goliath.

Not surprisingly, Saul is astonished that this young lad should
offer to fight the giant (v. 33), but David is determined and his courage comes from a simple logic: God has protected him in his shep-
herding work against the wild animals and he will do the same
against Goliath (vv. 34–37).

Though we know the story so well, we can still feel the tension as
this young man approaches the Philistine. David's strong words ring
out from the pages of scripture still: 'I come to you in the name of
the Lord of hosts' (v. 45). In that name he overpowers his foe, despite
the odds being stacked against him. Courage is the power from
within us that enables us to do things that would normally terrify us.
David would tell us that this power is best resourced from an uncom-
promising trust in God. David is a good guide for all who feel overwhelmed by the terrors of this world.

When my fears threaten to overwhelm me, grant me a David heart,
O Lord.

MICHAEL MITTON

The confident response

His eldest brother Eliab heard him talking to the men; and Eliab's anger was kindled against David. He said, 'Why have you come down? With whom have you left those few sheep in the wilderness? I know your presumption and the evil of your heart; for you have come down just to see the battle.' David said, 'What have I done now? It was only a question.'

We stay with the Goliath story and one brief conversation between David and his brother Eliab. Family dynamics have changed little over the centuries and the influence of parents and siblings had their effects in David's day just as they do today. Eliab is Jesse's eldest and, when Samuel saw him, he assumed *he* was the one chosen by God to be the next king (1 Samuel 16:6), but God chose the youngest.

In today's passage, when David makes his way to the battlefront, Eliab is most indignant and claims to see evil in David's heart. It is an insight into how Eliab felt about his brother and makes us wonder if this is how the rest of the family felt about him, too. David could well have been swayed by this family resentment, but he shows remarkable confidence in response to Eliab's accusation. In the coming years, too, David experienced bitter resentment not only from Saul but also from his own son, Absalom (see his rebellion in 2 Samuel 15). Such bitterness in the hearts of those close to him must have been painful, yet we see an impressive stability and graciousness in David's heart.

David gets his bearings from God's view of him. In the Psalms, we catch sight of this, perhaps especially in Psalm 139. As we follow David in the complex stories of his career, we see someone who is very centred in God, and trusts him as the one who has searched him and known him. Eliab may say there is evil in David's heart, but, for David, the all-important thing is to discover what God sees. As Samuel made clear right at the start, the Lord 'looks on the heart' (1 Samuel 16:7). Clearly he saw good in David's.

How is your heart today?

MICHAEL MITTON

The therapy of music

And David came to Saul, and entered his service. Saul loved him greatly, and he became his armour-bearer. Saul sent to Jesse, saying, 'Let David remain in my service, for he has found favour in my sight.' And whenever the evil spirit from God came upon Saul, David took the lyre and played it with his hand, and Saul would be relieved and feel better, and the evil spirit would depart from him.

David's first contact with Saul comes about because he is a brilliant musician. Right after the story of David's anointing, we move to a dark story about Saul being afflicted by an evil spirit (1 Samuel 16:14). The writer tells us this is 'from the Lord' (v. 14) and the usual understanding of this phrase is that the spirits were under the control of God. Nonetheless, they deranged Saul and he knew he needed help. The recommended remedy for this malaise was music. Someone in Saul's court happened to have heard a young shepherd playing the lyre and, subsequently, David is brought into Saul's court to play songs that calm his soul. You get the impression that it is something about the way David plays the music that carries with it the therapeutic work of God. Initially the music soothed Saul, but as his heart grew more bitter, his appreciation of David's music turned to resentment. On one occasion, David is playing his lyre and Saul hurls a spear at him, which David just manages to dodge (1 Samuel 18:10–11).

As we shall see, David used his musical gifts in worship, but here you get the impression that there was a quality about David's playing which had a powerful impact on people's souls. There was a strong creative surge in David's heart that erupted in music. He was so attuned to God that the music carried with it a power to bless the open heart and challenge the closed one. We may not all be musical, but it is a good exercise sometimes to listen to music in an attentive way, for it can often be a route to God's healing and an inspiration for us.

Listen to a piece of music and let God minister to you through it.

MICHAEL MITTON

The wild worshipper

David danced before the Lord with all his might; David was girded with a linen ephod. So David and all the house of Israel brought up the ark of the Lord with shouting, and with the sound of the trumpet. As the ark of the Lord came into the city of David, Michal daughter of Saul looked out of the window, and saw King David leaping and dancing before the Lord; and she despised him in her heart.

David's love of music stayed with him throughout his life and he became a renowned songwriter, referred to as the 'sweet psalmist of Israel' (2 Samuel 23:1, KJV). It must have been wonderful to have this highly creative king producing the most stirring and thoughtful psalms that were so loved by the people and deemed to be so inspired that they were carefully recorded and used for public worship. Perhaps they were sometimes used very formally, as they are in some churches today. In today's passage, however, we see another side of David. There is nothing formal in his riotous act of worship here! After establishing Jerusalem as his city, David wants to bring the ark of the covenant to Jerusalem. It represents the powerful presence of God, evidenced not least by the disaster that befell Uzzah (6:7). Such is his delight in the presence of God that he lets rip in an enthusiastic, wild dance that not even the disapproval of Michal can dampen.

David's heart of worship can be seen in his prayer in 2 Samuel 7:18–29, which comes shortly after the ark has arrived. It is a prayer he utters after hearing a mighty word from God delivered through the prophet Nathan (vv. 5–16). Again David lights up, not dancing this time, but speaking wonderful words of praise. They include a petition for the blessing of the temple (to be built by Solomon), but it is essentially a flow of gutsy praise and thanksgiving. It is clear that praise and worship erupted from the deepest parts of David's heart. He teaches us that worship is far more than formal expressions—it is spontaneous, heartfelt and full of enthusiasm.

Where can you find opportunities to worship God with heartfelt freedom?

MICHAEL MITTON

The affectionate heart

When David had finished speaking to Saul, the soul of Jonathan was bound to the soul of David, and Jonathan loved him as his own soul... Then Jonathan made a covenant with David, because he loved him as his own soul. Jonathan stripped himself of the robe that he was wearing, and gave it to David, and his armour, and even his sword and his bow and his belt.

We return today to the time before David was king to note a quality that was truly impressive in David, which was his ability to form remarkably deep friendships. The friend in today's passage is Jonathan, the eldest son of Saul. Had God approved of a dynasty through Saul, Jonathan would have been the rightful heir, but it is clear from their earliest meetings that Jonathan sees the workings of God much more clearly in David than he does in his father and has no doubts that David has been called by God to be king. For David, this makes space for a very safe friendship based on trust and a common understanding of the will of God. Saul is threatened by the friendship and reprimands his son for it (1 Samuel 20:30), but it has no effect on Jonathan, who continues to love David with great devotion. The depth of friendship is seen touchingly on the occasion when they say goodbye to one another for almost the last time (1 Samuel 20:41). When Jonathan is killed, David goes into the deepest mourning and finds more poetic words to express his grief (2 Samuel 1:25).

Nowadays, eyebrows can be raised at such deep devotion between people of the same sex, and the nature of this relationship has indeed been scrutinised by many. You feel, however, for the writer of these stories, all that speculation would be missing the point, which is that David was so wonderfully human that he acknowledged his need for deep companionship and was not afraid to form strong friendships. He is an example of a confident humanity that is willing to dwell deeply with others.

Spend some moments thinking about your close friends
and praying for them.

MICHAEL MITTON

The inventive mind

David took these words to heart and was very much afraid of King
Achish of Gath. So he changed his behaviour before them; he pre-
tended to be mad when in their presence. He scratched marks on the
doors of the gate, and let his spittle run down his beard. Achish said
to his servants, 'Look, you see the man is mad; why then have you
brought him to me?'

This is a curious story in a potentially dangerous situation, occurring
in the days of Saul's jealousy of David, when he is seeking to kill him.
David decides it is safer in Philistine territory than in Saul's kingdom,
so he seeks refuge in the company of Achish, the King of Gath. David
assumes nobody will know him in these parts, but, to his surprise
and dismay, his reputation has gone before him and the servants twig
that he is the increasingly famous David, who is proving a far greater
force than Saul (v. 11). Suddenly the world that David thought would
be safe becomes highly dangerous and his life is at risk. So, what does
David do? He appeals to his latent amateur dramatic skills and feigns
insanity. He is so convincing that Achish is completely taken in and
refuses to believe that this madman might be a threat.

I suppose you could argue that David was being devious and
deceptive here, but I think most would agree he was being highly
inventive. Faced with a serious threat to his life, he shows extraordi-
nary calm and presence of mind. He also manages to act insane with
great conviction. No doubt, when relating this tale to others, David
would have credited the Lord with aiding him at this time.

There is something encouraging in this story for us. Hopefully we
will never be in such a serious situation, but the Holy Spirit is a creative spirit. When we hit pressures of different kinds, he may well call
us to draw on talents we did not even know we had in our lives.
Times of pressure can be times of discovering new gifts that God has
given us.

Have there been moments of pressure in your life that have revealed
new talents?

MICHAEL MITTON

The listening heart

Now they told David, 'The Philistines are fighting against Keilah, and are robbing the threshing-floors.' David enquired of the Lord, 'Shall I go and attack these Philistines?' The Lord said to David, 'Go and attack the Philistines and save Keilah.' But David's men said to him, 'Look, we are afraid here in Judah; how much more then if we go to Keilah against the armies of the Philistines?' Then David enquired of the Lord again. The Lord answered him, 'Yes, go down to Keilah; for I will give the Philistines into your hand.'

In 1 Samuel 23 we get an insight into David's discipline of listening to God. By now it has become second nature to take his concerns to the Lord and listen for his response. In verse 6, there is a reference to the ephod. One of the official ways of listening to God at that time was to consult the Urim and Thummim, which were connected with the ephod and a divinely ordained means of communication with God (see Exodus 28:30). Thus, at the beginning of this chapter we have a typical example of David's listening. He gets the news that the Philistines are attacking Keilah, a city in the lowlands of Judah. Before rushing into battle, he enquires of the Lord and hears the reply that they should fight them. They go to battle and are successful, vindicating David's ability to hear God. When Saul hears the news, he plans to trap David in the city and, once again, David takes the time to listen to God (1 Samuel 23:9–12). We see other examples of this discipline throughout David's reign (such as 2 Samuel 2:1).

Saul was also committed to listening to God, but, towards the end of his life, he was finding there was no response to his enquiries (1 Samuel 28:6). In frustration, he decided to gain direction by consulting with the dead, which was against the law (see Leviticus 19:31). David and Saul thus become two very different models of leader—Saul's soul has become so corrupted that he seeks guidance via divination, whereas David's heart is humble and has remained open to God, so he is able to hear him.

How do you enquire of the Lord (1 Samuel 23:2)?

MICHAEL MITTON

The deceptive heart

It happened, late one afternoon, when David rose from his couch and was walking about on the roof of the king's house, that he saw from the roof a woman bathing; the woman was very beautiful. David sent someone to enquire about the woman. It was reported, 'This is Bathsheba daughter of Eliam, the wife of Uriah the Hittite.' So David sent messengers to fetch her, and she came to him, and he lay with her.

There is one low point in the life of King David that occurs around ten years after he is established in Jerusalem. It begins with an evening walk and a fateful glance, then develops into adultery and murder. In fact, David succeeds in breaking the sixth, seventh, ninth and tenth commandments (Exodus 20:13–17). As public falls from grace go, it is fairly spectacular! You get the sense from the way the story is written, however, that the worst of David's crimes is his attempt to deceive God and his people. He had somehow hoped that they would all be taken in by his cunning plan to avoid being discovered. At the end of chapter 11 you can almost hear David's sigh of relief that the plan has worked as he brings Bathsheba into his house and cares for her during her pregnancy. Come chapter 12, however, there is a knock at the door and in walks the prophet Nathan, who tells a story that reveals David's guilt. This is followed by the pronouncement of calamity (vv. 11–12), which is relatively lenient, given that the punishment for adultery at the time was death (Leviticus 20:10).

There is something impressive about the way the writer of the story of David candidly tells us about this humiliating episode in his life. It is like we are being told that even the great and wonderful are as vulnerable as the rest of us in this world. The message for all is that we cannot hide from God and we cannot deceive him. As the story progresses, we see there is a note of grace here—God is not ultimately concerned with punishment, but with restoration.

Father, grant me such confidence in your love that I will
never want to deceive you.

MICHAEL MITTON

The contrite heart

A Psalm of David, when the prophet Nathan came to him, after he had gone in to Bathsheba. Have mercy on me, O God, according to your steadfast love; according to your abundant mercy blot out my transgressions. Wash me thoroughly from my iniquity, and cleanse me from my sin. For I know my transgressions, and my sin is ever before me. Against you, you alone, have I sinned, and done what is evil in your sight.

As soon as Nathan has exposed David's sin and deception, David admits his guilt (2 Samuel 12:13) and makes no excuses. Psalm 51 is understood to be David's beautiful and sincere expression of guilt. It reveals the inner workings of his heart. At the outset he declares God's unfailing love (v. 1) and the penitential words that follow are held in the context of this love that seeks to restore rather than condemn. This whole shameful episode has given David a new awareness of the mercy of God that heals his shame. David is very aware that he has sinned (v. 3): there is no question of 'it does not really matter'. David is very clear that this sin business does matter (vv. 3–5) and his capacity for sin is all too evident in his humanity. What is important for David, though, is that God desires 'truth in the inward being' (v. 6). He has learned that he cannot deceive God. By being honest he can receive the great treasure of 'wisdom in my secret heart' (v. 6). What comes over so clearly in this psalm is the power of God to repair the soul. All that is required is a 'broken and contrite heart' (v. 17). Moreover, David can use this experience of personal failure to teach others about the merciful ways of God (v. 13).

The contrite heart is one that grasps the power of the redemptive nature of God's work. God did repair David and even blessed his relationship with Bathsheba. It was certainly not God's 'Plan A', but, because of the dynamics of his mercy, this union produced Solomon—one of the wisest people ever.

Read through Psalm 51 slowly and let the power of God's mercy touch your heart today.

MICHAEL MITTON

The warrior heart

David gathered all the people together and went to Rabbah, and fought against it and took it. He took the crown of Milcom from his head; the weight of it was a talent of gold, and in it was a precious stone; and it was placed on David's head. He also brought forth the spoil of the city, a very great amount. He brought out the people who were in it, and set them to work with saws and iron picks and iron axes, or sent them to the brickworks. Thus he did to all the cities of the Ammonites.

David's military achievements were, by any reckoning, remarkable. In today's passage we have one of his many victories—this time over the neighbouring Ammonites. Little by little, David subdued the Philistines (2 Samuel 8:1) and the neighbouring states, including Moab (2 Samuel 8:2) and Edom (2 Samuel 8:13). He also made treaties with the Phoenicians (2 Samuel 5:11–12). His wars therefore completed the conquest begun by Joshua and he secured all the borders of Israel. He had transformed Israel into the foremost power of the region and, by the standards of the day, it was a sizeable empire. Even before he became king, David proved himself to be a very competent warrior and, in the days when he was a threat to Saul, the cry went up among the peoples, 'Saul has killed his thousands, and David his tens of thousands' (1 Samuel 21:11).

Nowadays, we are likely to feel very uncomfortable about all this violence and bloodshed. Certainly under the new covenant Jesus shows no support for violence of this kind, even resisting the use of the sword at his arrest (Luke 22:49–51). Under the old covenant, though, these battles were a part of life and David was clearly a very capable and shrewd tactician as well as a courageous fighter. Further, in his early days, his army was made up of those who were 'in distress… in debt… discontented' (1 Samuel 22:2). You get the sense that there was something in David's style of leadership that was remarkably transforming and life in his army could bring out the best in people.

Spend a few moments praying for people of faith caught up in warfare.

MICHAEL MITTON

The honourable heart

Mephibosheth son of Jonathan son of Saul came to David, and fell on his face and did obeisance. David said, 'Mephibosheth!' He answered, 'I am your servant.' David said to him, 'Do not be afraid, for I will show you kindness for the sake of your father Jonathan; I will restore to you all the land of your grandfather Saul, and you yourself shall eat at my table always.' He did obeisance and said, 'What is your servant, that you should look upon a dead dog such as I am?'

During the final years of Saul's reign, David remains unfailingly respectful of the king and refuses to harm him even when he has an opportunity (1 Samuel 24). As we have seen, he was devoted to Saul's son, Jonathan. When they are both killed on Mount Gilboa, David deeply grieves for them both (2 Samuel 1:17–27). David has pledged to Jonathan to care for his family (1 Samuel 20:15, 42), despite the fact that any relative in this family could try to mount a challenge to his throne. Less honourable leaders may well have gone back on their word.

Jonathan had a son called Mephibosheth, who was five years old at the time of his father's death and was lame in both feet, following an injury he sustained at that time when his nurse dropped him while fleeing Jerusalem (2 Samuel 4:4). This injury would not have prevented him from mounting a challenge to David had he been minded to do so, but David refuses to see him as a threat and is more interested in honouring his word. As it happens, Mephibosheth proves himself to be genuinely humble. David honours him greatly by allowing him to regularly eat at his table (9:11). The love he had for Jonathan flows on to his son. There is something reassuringly secure in David's heart that allows him to honour this commitment to a friend and trust both Mephibosheth and God that this commitment will not become a threat to his reign. A culture of honour has a wonderful habit of disempowering our fears and bringing out the best in us and others.

Is God calling you to honour anyone today?

MICHAEL MITTON

The latter years

As soon as he had finished speaking, the king's sons arrived, and raised their voices and wept; and the king and all his servants also wept very bitterly. But Absalom fled, and went to Talmai son of Ammihud, king of Geshur. David mourned for his son day after day. Absalom, having fled to Geshur, stayed there for three years. And the heart of the king went out, yearning for Absalom; for he was now consoled over the death of Amnon.

Though David lived to old age, his declining years were not peaceful ones, for they were marred by growing anxieties about the succession to the throne. David had been so successful as king that he proved to be a hard act to follow and some of his sons clearly did not have their father's qualities. Absalom, for example, David's son by an Aramean princess (2 Samuel 3:3), became a serious problem. His sister had been raped by Amnon, David's eldest son, but David took no action regarding this terrible crime. Resentment built up in Absalom and he eventually has Amnon murdered (13:28). David was horrified at the murder of his firstborn son and lamented the exile of Absalom, who eventually returned to make a challenge for the throne that resulted in his death (2 Samuel 15 and 18). Adonijah, another son, also made an unsuccessful bid for the throne (1 Kings 1:1–27), but David had supposedly promised Bathsheba that Solomon would be his successor (vv. 13, 17). So David promptly made him king (vv. 28–48) and Adonijah gave up his attempt (v. 53).

The troubles of David's final years suggest that an area of weakness in him was to do with his family relationships. In retrospect, he might well have wished he had spent more time with his family—a longing that has resonated with many a spiritual leader since. We are all called to serve the Lord, but there are times when part of that service is to those in our own homes and families, who need us to offer them some time and good-quality listening.

---

*Lord, bless all who are part of my family and help me to give
time to any who need me today.*

MICHAEL MITTON

The heart of faith

It is you who light my lamp; the Lord, my God, lights up my darkness. By you I can crush a troop, and by my God I can leap over a wall. This God—his way is perfect; the promise of the Lord proves true; he is a shield for all who take refuge in him. For who is God except the Lord? And who is a rock besides our God?—the God who girded me with strength, and made my way safe. He made my feet like the feet of a deer, and set me secure on the heights.

The writer of our stories of David decided to insert Psalm 18 just prior to the 'last words of David' (2 Samuel 23:1). Though it was written a while before his death, it is placed here as it was reckoned to be of real significance and it is an apt summary of the heart of faith that was so evident in David's life. The psalm exults in a God, who protects his servants even when death threatens (Psalm 18:4–5), for he is a magnificent God who causes the earth to quake (v. 7) and rides on the wings of the wind (v. 10). Though he is mighty, he also reaches down tenderly to his people (v. 16) and takes note of a righteous heart (v. 20). Today's verses summarise the main theme of the psalm—the rock-like qualities of the Lord, who gives us strength and keeps us safe in a dangerous world. He does not just protect us, he also empowers us for adventure and leads us up to the high places of vision and freedom.

Psalm 18 ends with cries of praise (vv. 46–50) and you can almost see David with tambourine and ephod, high-kicking his way into Jerusalem, beside himself with love for his Lord. Ultimately, it was this love that inspired and drove him, rescued and delivered him. He was undoubtedly one of the best, for he lived close to God and managed to avoid the seductions of power that poisoned the hearts of so many of his successors. His bold yet vulnerable witness shines brilliantly from these history books.

What have you loved most about the character of David?

MICHAEL MITTON

The Son of David

A very large crowd spread their cloaks on the road, and others cut branches from the trees and spread them on the road. The crowds that went ahead of him and that followed were shouting, 'Hosanna to the Son of David! Blessed is the one who comes in the name of the Lord! Hosanna in the highest heaven!' When he entered Jerusalem, the whole city was in turmoil, asking, 'Who is this?' The crowds were saying, 'This is the prophet Jesus from Nazareth in Galilee.'

Matthew begins his Gospel with 'An account of the genealogy of Jesus the Messiah, the son of David, the son of Abraham' (1:1), thus establishing a strong connection between Jesus and David from the start of his account. This connection with David crops up a few times in the Gospels, where Jesus is called the 'Son of David' (see, for example, Matthew 9:27). When Jesus heals a demonised man the crowds ask eagerly, 'Can this be the Son of David?' (Matthew 12:23). This term 'Son of David' had become by this time a recognised term for the Messiah, but it is interesting that some people should use it in preference to 'Messiah' or other established terms. All this reaches a crescendo at the animated celebration when Jesus enters Jerusalem on the donkey, which makes people think immediately of the promises of the coming Messiah in passages such as Zechariah 9:9. In the thousand years between David and Jesus, there had developed a very strong belief that the Messiah would be firmly linked to the great King David.

Jesus must have spent many hours reading the stories of David and studying his character, as we have been doing these past two weeks. Jesus did not share David's failings, but there is, nonetheless, a 'family likeness' about his heart of faith, love, wisdom and courage. Did David maybe catch a glimpse of his great descendant? Perhaps he did in some of his high moments of worship and praise. One thing is for sure, if he were to visit this world today, his great desire would be to draw people's gaze to the Son of God.

Where do you see comparisons between the lives of Jesus and David?

MICHAEL MITTON

Feasting in the New Testament

Then the kingdom of heaven shall be likened to ten virgins who took their lamps and went out to meet the bridegroom… And at midnight a cry was heard: 'Behold, the bridegroom is coming; go out to meet him!' (Matthew 25:1, 6, NKJV).

When the hour came, Jesus took his place at the table with the apostles. He said to them, 'I have wanted so much to eat this Passover meal with you before I suffer! For I tell you, I will never eat it until it is given its full meaning in the Kingdom of God' (Luke 22:14–16, GNB).

All around the world, families and communities celebrate special events with a feast. Birth, marriage, coronation, death, anniversaries, coming of age, opening a place of worship—these and all kinds of significant occasions are marked by people gathering, dressed in their best, sharing food and drink, ceremonial, music and maybe dancing.

Faith is about our life set within the cosmic dimension of mystery; it explores and interprets the meaning and significance of human experience. In his life and teaching, too, Jesus links the basic and simple realities of everyday eating and drinking with the majestic greater reality of the kingdom of heaven.

The beating heart of this theme is located in its twin characteristics of joy and hospitality. Christianity is a mystical religion, but nonetheless emphasises neighbourliness, love and belonging. It offers a vision for the creation of inclusive community. Jesus' parables of the kingdom and the sketching in Acts and the epistles of the church's development encourage us to see how heaven can be brought to earth. By responding to God's invitation, putting one another before ourselves, lovingly including and providing for the poor and needy, we set the feast and celebrate our faith in God as Father of all humankind.

Therefore let us keep the feast, not with old leaven, neither with the leaven of malice and wickedness; but with the unleavened bread of sincerity and truth (1 Corinthians 5:8, KJV).

Unite us all around one table, O Lord, we pray; for have we not all one Father, did not one God create us?

PENELOPE WILCOCK

A feast of redemption

'What are they like?... "We played the pipe for you, and you did not dance; we sang a dirge, and you did not cry." For John the Baptist came neither eating bread nor drinking wine, and you say, "He has a demon." The Son of Man came eating and drinking, and you say, "Here is a glutton and a drunkard, a friend of tax collectors and sinners."'

Jesus confronts the reality that there is no pleasing some people. They bring a 'heads I win, tails you lose' mentality to every conceivable situation. They thought John was crazy because he was an ascetic and they think Jesus is a slob because wherever he goes the party happens. As Jesus put it, 'What are they like?' (v. 31b).

The feasting that seemed to accompany Jesus everywhere he went, whether supper at Martha and Mary's place or afternoon tea with Zacchaeus, was not about the food and drink. I am not sure if his critics failed to see this or they were refusing to acknowledge the real issue because it showed them up in a very unfavourable light.

The parties that sprang up around Jesus were the bubbling over of gratitude and joy. Lazarus raised from the dead. Zacchaeus the social reject given an offer of unconditional friendship from the most popular prophet in town. Feasts are about celebration and—unlike their established religious leaders—Jesus gave people something to celebrate. If you are healed, forgiven, cleansed, renewed, restored, how can you help rejoicing? He brought them the jubilee of the Lord, the feast of redemption. Spontaneously, in heartfelt gratitude, in the heady and effervescent atmosphere of a new chance, as Jesus restored to them health and hope they thought was gone for ever, the people celebrated. This was like winning the lottery, but better.

The coming of Jesus is the signal for the party to start. In his presence, joy is not only appropriate but it is also inevitable.

PENELOPE WILCOCK

A feast of astonishing provision

They took him [the man in charge] the water, which now had turned into wine, and he tasted it. He did not know where this wine had come from (but, of course, the servants who had drawn out the water knew); so he called the bridegroom and said to him, 'Everyone else serves the best wine first, and after the guests have had plenty to drink, he serves the ordinary wine. But you have kept the best wine until now!'

My friend Margery loved blackberries and grew them in her garden. She ate them with ice-cream. The main crop comes in September, but Margery observed a first wave ripening in August. They were the biggest and juiciest of all—the first fruits. The quality tailed off from then on. Jewish law required the people to bring tithes of everything to God—not leftovers, but the first and best of their harvest, the biggest and juiciest.

In this wedding feast at Cana in Galilee, there is a correlation, a reciprocity, between our giving to each other or God and his giving to us. It is a demonstration of lavish, laughing generosity—a celebration of loving abundance, because the miracle occurs when they are on to the dregs. All they had has gone—run out.

Here is a Lord who understands what is important to us—saving us from humiliation. Jesus could have said, 'Run out? Be glad you have water. It's good for you. You should not drink so much anyway', but no, he inspires the response, 'You have kept the best wine until now.'

I have seen such a miracle in hospice care. Sometimes in those last few weeks, as the time rather than wine is running out, I have known people say that they never really lived, never really loved until now. Hope is never gone, because Jesus travels with us. Whatever our circumstances, the abundance of his provision continues to astonish and delight us.

'Even to your old age and grey hairs I am he, I am he who will sustain you. I have made you and I will carry you; I will sustain you and I will rescue you' (Isaiah 46:4, NIV). O God of all grace, you know my need and your love will provide for me. I put my trust in you.

PENELOPE WILCOCK

A feast that comes through us

That evening his disciples came to him and said, 'It is already very late, and this is a lonely place. Send the people away and let them go to the villages to buy food for themselves.' 'They don't have to leave,' answered Jesus. 'You yourselves give them something to eat!' 'All we have here are five loaves and two fish,' they replied. 'Then bring them here to me,' Jesus said.

Back in the early 1980s when John Wimber came to England to teach about signs and wonders, I heard him speak on this miracle. In his funny, vivid, inimitable way, looking up at the tiered seating in the conference hall, packed to capacity and holding about 5000 people, he became first Jesus, saying, 'You feed 'em!', then one of the disciples, cupping in his hand a morsel of bread and a fish head, looking up in slow apprehension at the hungry crowds, saying, 'Who? Me?'

It was Wimber who brought to my attention that in this miracle the provision came by the power of God in Jesus, but through the disciples. Without their participation, action, distribution, the crowd would have stayed unfed.

When they brought what they had to Jesus, he blessed it by giving thanks, shared it out between the disciples and they fed the people. In so doing, they also had enough for their own supper.

This is the circulation of miraculous power—our trust in God and his trust in us. We act in faith with whatever we have to hand. Notice, too, the crucial role of gratitude, so Jesus, tasked with feeding 5000 people, holds up his five loaves and two fish to God and says not, 'What the dickens am I meant to do with this?' but 'Thank you.'

To a needy world, I have so little to offer. I cannot see how it will ever be enough. Yet, I lift up what I have to you, God of miracles, and I put my faith in you. Thank you; you never fail me.

PENELOPE WILCOCK

A feast of forgetfulness

When the festival was over, they started back home, but the boy Jesus stayed in Jerusalem. His parents did not know this; they thought that he was with the group, so they travelled a whole day and then started looking for him among their relatives and friends. They did not find him, so they went back to Jerusalem looking for him. On the third day they found him.

You could find Jesus at a feast. You could also lose him there.

A wonderful word has travelled, to our great enrichment, from the Buddhist faith tradition into the Christian tradition: mindfulness. It is about bringing your attention to your responsibilities and your chosen way in all circumstances, not allowing yourself to be distracted. The story is told of a young monk walking through the rain to see his spiritual advisor, excitedly anticipating the forthcoming tutorial. When he comes into his mentor's presence, the wise old man asks him, 'When you entered the porch, and took off your sandals, did you leave your umbrella to the left of them or to the right?' The young monk thought about it, but could not remember. To his great disappointment, his teacher said only, 'Then that is your lesson for today.'

Our faithfulness is practised in the little things, the daily responsibilities. In all the rush and bustle of events and circumstances, it is so easy to be distracted—to snap instead of answer courteously, do a botched and hurried job, completely fail to notice someone else's suffering. Sometimes we chase trails of worry about the future, nostalgia or resentment about the past, leaving the present moment unattended to. We lose sight of Jesus. 'Oh, what? I though he was with you!'

For the Christian disciple, staying faithful is about keeping an eye on Jesus all the time, even when there is a lot going on.

'Blessed are they that keep his testimonies, and that seek him with the whole heart' (Psalm 119:2, KJV). This day, Master, help me to keep my eyes fixed on you. If ever I lose sight of you, come quickly and take me by the hand.

PENELOPE WILCOCK

A feast for the lost and found

'Which one of you, having a hundred sheep and losing one of them, does not leave the ninety-nine in the wilderness and go after the one that is lost until he finds it? When he has found it, he lays it on his shoulders and rejoices. And when he comes home, he calls together his friends and neighbours, saying to them, "Rejoice with me, for I have found my sheep that was lost."'

Reading the Gospels, context is all. This story of the lost sheep is preceded by a comment that tax-collectors and sinners were drawing near to listen to Jesus, making the religious elite grumble, 'This man welcomes sinners and eats with them.'

Then, after the passage, comes the story of the woman who lost a coin, lit a lamp and swept the house, searching, sharp-eyed and determined, until she found it. Then she threw a party because she was so glad and relieved to have it back. In this, chapter 15 of his Gospel, known as his 'chapter of the lost', Luke delineates God's heart of loving kindness. 'Just so, I tell you,' Jesus says, 'there is joy in the presence of the angels of God over one sinner who repents' (15:10).

This speaks comfort and encouragement to us who know we are lost, who acknowledge the hopelessness of attempting perfection and are pinning all our hopes on a God who loves us enough to stoop down and gather us to him. It has another gift besides that. To have lost something implies it does (still) belong to you. These stories of losing and finding are not about discovery, but reconciliation. The community of the redeemed knows itself not only as forgiven and loved by God but also as originally belonging to him, too. In Christ, we come home to ourselves.

Jesus, Good Shepherd, thank you for caring about me, wanting me. Thank you for looking for me, rescuing me. I trust you to lead me home.

PENELOPE WILCOCK

A feast of new life

Then the son said to him, '… I am no longer worthy to be called your son.' But the father said to his slaves, 'Quickly, bring out a robe—the best one—and put it on him; put a ring on his finger and sandals on his feet. And get the fatted calf and kill it, and let us eat and celebrate; for this son of mine was dead and is alive again; he was lost and is found!' And they began to celebrate.

Lovers of words cannot seem to agree completely on the etymological roots of the word 'repent'. Some insist it grew out of the Latin word for 'penitent' and is all about sorrow for sin committed. The New Testament is in Greek, however, and the Greek word for 'repent' means to turn around—to do an about face. It was a military term for soldiers on the march doing a 180 degree turn to get going in the opposite direction. That Greek word is *metanoia*, signifying a change of mind of such significance that it involves transformation of a person's whole inner nature, expressed in our passage by the contrasting of dead and alive, lost and found.

The story does not lose sight of the need to say sorry, to honestly and humbly seek forgiveness, which is part and parcel of repentance. It does, however, bring out the grace and generosity of God, who wastes no time on scoldings or 'I told you so' diatribes but gets straight to work on developing the potential of a new beginning. The work of God in Jesus is about making all things new—not a factory of novelties but a healing of the broken. The relief and joy and gratitude this brings is the root of Christian celebration. This party, this feast, is all about love and restoration.

Father, in prayer I come home to you again, in love and trust, in hope and confidence. Forgive me, lift from me my burden of sin. Fill me anew with your spirit of life, joy and peace. O Lord, I receive your love.

PENELOPE WILCOCK

A feast that is always available to us

'Listen! For all these years I have been working like a slave for you, and I have never disobeyed your command; yet you have never given me even a young goat so that I might celebrate with my friends. But when this son of yours came back... you killed the fatted calf for him!' Then the father said to him, 'Son, you are always with me, and all that is mine is yours.'

Uh oh. The prodigal son has a brother.

Preachers focus, understandably, on the effervescent joy of being forgiven, on the God who holds out the opportunity of starting again. That is certainly both relevant and welcome, but when the elder brother is mentioned, it is usually with opprobrium—focusing on his jealousy, sourness and so on. Sensing which way the wind is blowing, the members of the congregation try desperately to pretend that they identify more with the prodigal son, and his sex, drugs and rock 'n' roll lifestyle, than they do with the sober, faithful, responsible older brother. As if!

This would not be the gospel, though, if it were good news for only one section of the community. The father in Jesus' story has the same abundant love and generosity for his older boy, too: 'Son... all that is mine is yours' (v. 31). Think about that for a minute. Is that mind-blowing or have I missed something?

This is not a special-occasion God, a few high points interspersed in a long bleak trudge through the valleys. Our Father in heaven offers us joy for the everyday. It is the will of God that we allow ourselves to have fun, have some treats, that we should have the confidence and trust to reach out for what makes us happy. Hard to believe, I know, for those of us brought up with anxiety and guilt, but that is what the story says.

'In your presence there is fullness of joy; at your right hand are pleasures for evermore' (Psalm 16:11, ESV). Give me the grace, O God, to live in the fullness of your love. May the abundance of your kindness fill my life and overflow to bless everyone I meet.

PENELOPE WILCOCK

A feast with an RSVP

The Kingdom of heaven is like this. Once there was a king who prepared a wedding feast for his son. He sent his servants to tell the
invited guests to come to the feast, but they did not want to come. So
he sent other servants with this message for the guests: 'My feast is
ready now; my bullocks and prize calves have been butchered, and
everything is ready. Come to the wedding feast!' But the invited
guests paid no attention.

I grew up in a poor family living in a rich village with some very
wealthy neighbours. How my mother treasured invitations to take
tea with refined ladies in large houses, giving pride of place on the
mantelpiece to the elegant printed cards with their copperplate let-
tering! The message always ended R.S.V.P., which my mother
explained meant 'répondez s'il vous plaît'—that is, a reply was necessary. To ignore the invitation would be the height of discourtesy.

Today's passage sketches a picture of a king who wants to include
us all in the joyous wedding feast for his son. Not just the 'in crowd',
everyone invited, nobody left out. This exciting celebration of life is
supposed to be the highlight of our lives and we do not even have to
wait, counting off the days. It is starting now—the party is ready! It
seems almost incomprehensible that, for some people, this is of no
account and the king's invitation is treated like a flyer through the
door for cheap pizza on Tuesdays—straight in the recycling bin or
trampled on the doormat.

I guess it is all too easy to be so focused on the mundane that we
miss the invitation to heaven. Have you responded? See you there?

---

*Your Majesty, my Master and my most royal Lord, I thank you with all
my heart for remembering me, including me, inviting me. Today, I am
saying, 'Yes, please!' to everything, so proud and so pleased am I to be
numbered among your guests at this wonderful celebration.*

PENELOPE WILCOCK

A feast worthy of our best

So the servants went out into the streets and gathered all the people they could find, good and bad alike; and the wedding hall was filled with people. The king... saw a man who was not wearing wedding clothes. 'Friend, how did you get in here without wedding clothes?' the king asked him. But the man said nothing. Then the king told the servants, 'Tie him up hand and foot, and throw him outside.'

Jesus makes it clear that 'Everyone is welcome' is not the same as 'Anything goes'.

My daughter worked for a confident, influential landowner who, passing through London one day, suggested they drop in at the Ritz for tea. Unfortunately they were wearing jeans. The concierge did not care who they were—there is a dress code at the Ritz; entry was forbidden to them. They had to settle for the Savoy.

The implication of our Bible passage—that heaven has a dress code, too—has provoked much scholarly speculation. A consensus has been reached that the required wedding garment is God's forgiveness. It seems to me that, much like the Ritz, you do not need a designer budget to get in—they will not look down their noses at you—but you are expected to prepare and present yourself appropriately. There is the glorious and lavish part that God does, his mercy—like the Ritz with its gold-leafed cherubs, fountain and rich carpets, pristine starched table linen and dainty finger sandwiches. Then there is the modest but essential part that we do in response—the cleansing of our souls in his redeeming love and the adornment of our lives in habits of modesty, peace, gentleness, prayer and loving kindness.

This is not spiritual snobbery, it is about keeping life beautiful for everyone.

Lord Jesus, I humbly acknowledge my insufficiency, poverty of being and wretched rags of self-righteousness. Help me start again. Strip me, wash me, clothe me in the beauty of compassion, slip my feet into the shoes of the gospel of peace. Make me fit to come into your presence.

PENELOPE WILCOCK

76

A feast meant to be shared

A rich man... splendidly clothed in purple and fine linen... lived each day in luxury. At his gate lay a poor man named Lazarus who was covered with sores. As Lazarus lay there longing for scraps from the rich man's table, the dogs would come and lick his open sores. Finally, the poor man died and was carried by the angels to be with Abraham. The rich man also died and was buried, and his soul went to the place of the dead.

Political parties differ in their approaches to the poor and needy. Some take all wealth into state administration, creating equality of citizens; others protect family dynasties of inheritance, promoting a trickling down of wealth via employment and charity.

Unfortunately, you cannot legislate for kindness and compassion. Communist regimes are as elitist as aristocracies.

The gospel is political in that it is always about community. This feast is not a banquet you eat alone in front of the telly, the door bolted, the curtains drawn; it is for sharing. Loving your neighbours implies seeing them, knowing them. Yet, the gospel cannot be appropriated by party politics because anything partisan promotes self-interest and the gospel is not about even the self-interest of the poor; it is about loving my neighbour. This means responding to every kind of poverty and vulnerability with the gentleness of compassion. Its currency is quite different from the coinage of money and status, even of education and medical care. Its kindness may flow through those channels, but they are not the gospel itself. The love of God is implemented not by systems but by the free choice of a human being.

'Speak up for people who cannot speak for themselves. Protect the rights of all who are helpless. Speak for them and be a righteous judge. Protect the rights of the poor and needy' (Proverbs 31:8–10, GNB). Help me, loving Father, to see Christ in everyone I meet. May I be neither overawed by status nor scornful of lowliness. Make me compassionate towards all who are vulnerable, remembering that each one is infinitely precious in your sight.

PENELOPE WILCOCK

A feast of faith and hope

Then he took a cup, and when he had given thanks, he gave it to them, saying, 'Drink from it, all of you. This is my blood of the covenant, which is poured out for many for the forgiveness of sins. I tell you, I will not drink from this fruit of the vine from now on until that day when I drink it new with you in my Father's kingdom.'

I take my hat off to Jesus. Such unshakeable faith. Such far-sighted-ness. Such insight and vision. He lifts up the cup to God of his own blood soon to be shed—a cocktail of fear and agony, torture and death—and he gives thanks!

Thanksgiving blesses, effects transformation. He knows that in this rich wine, this bitter medicine, spilled blood, lies the hope of humanity, the way forward to a new creation. By this blessing we become blood relatives; here is effected our belonging to him, our chance to benefit from his sacrifice and be forgiven. He also raises our everyday sustenance, the ordinary components of human life, into the sacred realm, making them holy. With such surpassing cour-age and grace, he looks beyond the worst that this world can do to him, to the coming of a kingdom of wonder, love and peace; the harvest of this cup of suffering. In this feast, Jesus links together all that has wounded us with the hope he has won for us. This feast acknowledges the realities and limitations of human life while fixing it in the greater context of the brightness of God's coming kingdom of peace and joy.

Lord Jesus, I adore you in your unconditional self-offering. In this humble meal where you give all you have, I feast on your grace, your love. Today I give my life into your hands. Raise the cup with all it contains, say the blessing for me, so that I may feast eternally with you in the kingdom you are starting here on earth. Help me to give thanks today for so glorious a salvation.

PENELOPE WILCOCK

A feast requiring responsible planning

The Hellenists complained... because their widows were being neglected in the daily distribution of food. And the twelve called together the whole community of the disciples and said, 'It is not right that we should neglect the word of God in order to wait at tables... Select... seven men of good standing, full of the Spirit and of wisdom, whom we may appoint to this task, while we... devote ourselves to prayer and to serving the word.'

Eating together is a powerful and primal kind of bonding. When people sit down to eat, they are off guard, so trust is implied. Eating the same food creates cultural belonging. As our passage shows, from its first beginnings, the church regarded eating together as essential—even when it caused contention.

The practising of the Christian faith is organised around a meal table, of course—the sacred, solemn mystery of the Eucharist. Reading the Acts of the Apostles, it seems that the ritualised ceremonial meal, around which we unite today, was once an actual supper—a sharing of the daily bread and flask of wine that were the sustenance of ordinary people. In modern times, the Alpha course has focused our recognition of the importance of eating together, reviving the practice of incorporating a meal as an integral feature of fellowship, strengthening and clarifying the links between sacrament and ordinary daily life.

If loving our neighbour, living our faith, sharing in fellowship is to declare itself in practical, physical realities like this, organisation and finance are implied. The property management and administrative aspects of church that feel so tedious and not very spiritual turn out to be at the heart of something very beautiful after all.

God of love, help me to remember that in a life of holiness, you call me to not only beautiful symbolism but also practical, everyday reality.

He bids us build each other up; And, gathered into one,
To our high calling's glorious hope, We hand in hand go on.

Charles Wesley, 1747

PENELOPE WILCOCK

A feast of contentment

Jesus noticed how some of the guests were choosing the best places, so he told this parable to all of them: 'When someone invites you to a wedding feast, do not sit down in the best place. It could happen that someone more important than you has been invited, and your host, who invited both of you, would have to come and say to you, "Let him have this place."'

Twenty-first-century families! The parents of both bride and groom were divorced; both fathers had remarried. So, the bride's father's new wife was not invited (until later when her mother got a boyfriend) and the groom's father's new wife was not allowed to sit at the top table, but had to sit separately from her husband while the original couples were reunited at the top table. Complicated? Yes. The groom's father objected, the bride cried, and the groom did not speak to his father for two months.

The thing is, sometimes it is helpful to read Jesus' teachings about community and simple peace between human beings rather than those about religion. Think of our passage for today in those terms. Suppose we let go of attachment to social precedence, forget about our rights and what is due to us, choose not to be offended, to see things from the other person's point of view? This, says Jesus, is the way in to the kingdom of heaven.

At times of family tension, my husband quotes Tom Clancy's words from *Debt of Honor* (HarperCollins, 1998): 'The Japanese are giving a war. Are we going?' Humility and contentment, the relinquishment of rights and status in favour of simple kindness—these are the building blocks of the peaceable kingdom.

'Let me be full, let me be empty, let me have all things, let me have nothing: I freely and wholeheartedly yield all things to your pleasure and disposal' (from the Methodist Covenant Prayer). Oh, my Master— call me and I will come. Show me where to be and I will go there. Give me my place in the world and I will be content. Only give me the grace to discern your voice and the faith to understand and follow.

PENELOPE WILCOCK

A feast in the eternal life of heaven

Then the angel said to me, 'Write this: Blessed are those who are invited to the wedding supper of the Lamb!' And he added, 'These are the true words of God.' At this I fell at his feet to worship him. But he said to me, 'Don't do that! I am a fellow servant with you and with your brothers and sisters who hold to the testimony of Jesus. Worship God!'

The marriage feast as a parable of the kingdom persists through the New Testament. As the infant church begins to develop the structures of its life in community, welcoming and inclusive shared meals provide the faithful sign of a hospitable God. Bearing in mind that in its early days the church suffered severe and violent persecution, one can see how the idea of the marriage feast comes to symbolise the brave celebration of unquenchable Christian hope.

In this last book of the Bible, written late by John on Patmos, the symbol of the marriage feast is impressed on us again. This time it brings a caution to settle for nothing less. As the visionary falls at the feet of the angel to worship him, he is reprimanded. God and God alone is worthy of worship. Everyone else, saints and angels and all the company of heaven, are the invited guests at the marriage feast of the one true Lord.

The message is clear. Fellowship, hospitality, respectful and humble love—these are the attitudes we must espouse towards one another in service of the servant king. Adulation and hierarchies have no part in our faith. We have one Lord only and our faith is in Christ crucified, risen and ascended. Our hope is in him.

This is the hour of banquet and of song;
this is the heavenly table spread for me;
here let me feast, and feasting, still prolong
the hallowed hour of fellowship with thee.

Horatius Bonar, 'Here, O my Lord, I see thee face to face' (1855)

PENELOPE WILCOCK

81

Spiritual gifts

'Now concerning spiritual gifts, brothers and sisters, I do not want you to be uninformed' (1 Corinthians 12:1, NRSV).

The spiritual life lies at the heart of the Christian life. Seeking to live according to God's will as revealed in and through the life, death and resurrection of Christ demands that, as Christians, we pay special attention to nourishing and strengthening our spiritual relationship with Christ. I would even go further and suggest that the chief function of the church is that of encouraging and equipping Christians to deepen their covenant with Christ and their experience of God.

Quintessentially, those who believe in God are called to experience God in all his richness and depth. Such experiencing far outweighs having correct theories about God. To experience God on such an intimate and personal level provides us with the means to embark on an exciting journey of faith. The journey is not actually about going further in a kind of linear way but, rather, going deeper into one's self. By doing so we are better able to participate in the life of Christ deeply and richly within our own hearts. My reading of several of Paul's letters suggests that this call (and challenge) to become one with Christ, so as to enter into and participate in the life of God, is high on his missionary agenda. 1 Corinthians 12:1 reveals his determination to do all he possibly can to enable the new Christians to recognise the significance of the spiritual life and manifold gifts that such a life can yield. I get the distinct impression that in chapter 12 Paul is probably responding to some enquiry from certain Corinthians as to the meaning of such spiritual gifts.

During the next two weeks, my aim is to explore Paul's list of gifts and use chapter 12:1–11 as a backdrop to exploring those same gifts elsewhere in the scriptures. I have categorised Paul's list of spiritual gifts under seven headings and examine the manifestation of those gifts elsewhere in the New Testament. I then follow each of them with a story from the Old Testament where similar such gifts are revealed.

ANDREW JONES

Wisdom and knowledge

Then the kingdom of heaven will be like this. Ten bridesmaids took their lamps and went to meet the bridegroom. Five of them were foolish, and five were wise. When the foolish took their lamps, they took no oil with them; but the wise took flasks of oil with their lamps.

Paul is clearly concerned about the unity of the fledgling Corinthian church, where divisions are already apparent. He wants them to know that Christians differ from each other and that uniformity of experience and ministry is not a realistic expectation. At the heart of unity lies the Spirit and it is the Spirit who bestows on Christians the various gifts needed to build up the community of Christ's followers.

Commentators on this passage differ as to the precise meaning of the various gifts, but, for me, 'wisdom' in Paul's context means evaluating realities in the light of God's grace and acting on those realities in response to it. 'Knowledge' is the insight into the real nature of the world as created by God. To utter knowledge, then, is to speak a word under inspiration, thus giving insight into life's realities to others. So, in this sense, both wisdom and knowledge are practical and realistic gifts given by the Spirit as we endeavour to deepen our spiritual life. Similarly, the ministry of Jesus is peppered with instances of realistic and practical wisdom and knowledge.

The picture painted of the bridesmaids here is very typical of a first-century Palestinian wedding. The wisdom and knowledge conveyed in the parable is, again, practical and realistic for people who believe in God. The point of the parable is that the disciples are to be prepared and ready when the Lord comes and, thus, enter the kingdom. The utterance of wisdom and knowledge in this passage comes at the end of the parable: 'Keep awake therefore, for you know neither the day nor the hour' (Matthew 25:13). Could it be that in saying, 'I do not want you to be uninformed' (1 Corinthians 12:1), Paul is actually saying the same as Jesus: 'Keep awake'?

Spirit of the risen Christ, give us today the grace to utter words of wisdom.

ANDREW JONES

Queen Esther reveals wisdom

'For if you keep silence at such a time as this, relief and deliverance will rise for the Jews from another quarter, but you and your father's family will perish. Who knows? Perhaps you have come to royal dignity for just such a time as this?'

The book of Esther is a tale of the lethal danger that faced Judaism at some time in the fifth century BC and the rise of an orphan in exile who became the most powerful woman in the Persian Empire. Quite unexpectedly, she uttered words of wisdom and knowledge and, through them, saved a nation. There are three aspects of her utterance of wisdom that I find particularly interesting. First, she rose to a position of prophetic prominence at a time of complete leadership meltdown. She was different in many ways from those around her—there was a freshness about her—and her utterance was distinctive. She reminded her community that everyone can make a difference.

Second, Esther was called on to perform particular tasks and to act where God placed her. She discovered her vocation deep in a place of crisis. Socially, she acted on behalf of the common people and identified herself fully with them. Ethically, she was fundamentally relational—she criss-crossed boundaries, mixed traditions and scotched taboos. Politically, as a woman, she was counter-cultural. Spiritually, she called for prayer and urged the people not to ask why danger had befallen them but explore new tools to cope with them.

Third, Esther had been prepared for her moment by her history—a history of conflict, tragedy, poverty, childhood as an orphan, hardship and obscurity. Her experiences were her preparation and Esther used her story to contribute to the making of a better world.

In his list of spiritual gifts, Paul does not simply list 'wisdom' and 'knowledge' in isolation, but prefaces both gifts with the word 'utterance'. The suggestion is that it is not sufficient simply to behave wisely and act knowledgeably but we need also to speak it and speak it constantly for the common good.

Who we are is God's gift to us; who we become is our gift to God .

ANDREW JONES

Faithfulness

In this you rejoice, even if now for a little while you have had to suffer various trials, so that the genuineness of your faith—being more precious than gold that, though perishable, is tested by fire—may be found to result in praise and glory and honour when Jesus Christ is revealed.

Peter's first letter is clearly a pastoral document in which he reminds the recipients that the Christian vocation is both precious and dignified. Peter describes the vocation in terms of it being a 'house' (1 Peter 2:5; 4:17) for the 'homeless' (1:17; 2:11) and his call to remain faithful runs throughout the letter. The context of the letter is one of persecution—Nero's violent persecution of Christians—and Christians were constantly in a precarious position in a threatening pagan world. Consequently, there was a real danger that, in the face of hostility, many Christians would abandon faith in Jesus Christ and revert to pagan ways. Peter encourages them to 'stand fast' (5:12) and exhorts them that those who are regarded by the world as aliens and strangers are able to find a 'home' in the Christian community. Faithfulness, then, was an integral part of the journey towards finding that 'home'.

In the Bible, we discover that the gift of faithfulness is essentially an interpersonal gift—people are faithful to an 'other'. Similarly, Christians are faithful to a God who constantly reveals himself as a faithful God (2 Corinthians 1:20; Revelation 3:14). Christians are consistently reassured in the New Testament that their faithfulness is sustained by God's unlimited faithfulness to his covenant—even to those who are unfaithful. This reminds us that the gift of faithfulness is directly related to responsibility. Those who are irresponsible will find it difficult to 'stand fast' and remain faithful. Genuine faithfulness is always faithfulness to an 'other', whether that is to another person or a community. Such faithfulness is a way of expressing love and accompanied by gratitude. As such, it becomes the authentic way in which the early Christians and us today are equipped to 'stand fast' in times of difficulty and in the face of temptation.

Without faithfulness no other virtue can flourish.

ANDREW JONES

Abraham responds in faith

Then the Lord appeared to Abram, and said, 'To your offspring I will give this land.' So he built there an altar to the Lord, who had appeared to him. From there he moved on to the hill country on the east of Bethel, and pitched his tent, with Bethel on the west and Ai on the east; and there he built an altar to the Lord and invoked the name of the Lord.

For me, the Old Testament really 'gets going' in the remarkable encounter between God and Abraham. He is probably the original key player in the whole of the Hebrew scriptures and, significantly, he emerges as a very faithful father figure in the Jewish, Christian and Muslim traditions—in all three he is portrayed as a man of dignity, firm in his faith, humane and respected by the people he encounters on his long journey across the Near Eastern world. He is the one who begins a line of crucial Old Testament figures—Abraham, Isaac, Jacob and the twelve sons, including Joseph.

Genesis, from which today's passage is taken, is primarily a book that seeks to record the story of a people's faithfulness and help keep that faithfulness alive and fresh, but always as a response to God's faithfulness and commitment to them. The main setting for the story of Abraham that we glimpse here is the central hill country in the land of Canaan, promised to him and his ancestors by God. As a mark of gratitude, faithfulness and acknowledgement of God as Lord of the land, Abraham built an altar. My reading of the Abraham stories—his journey, his encounters, his responses and his judgements—is one of freedom and of adventure. The kind of faithfulness he reveals is not one of simply responding to rules and regulations as if true and authentic faithfulness is merely prescribed by rubrics. Rather, Abraham's adventure began with a leap of faith steeped in mystery.

We live in a broken world that robs us of joyous adventure and mystery. It is also one where there are too many religious divisions. Abraham is the shared ancestor of Jews, Christians and Muslims; he holds the key to our deepest fears and our hopeful reconciliation.

ANDREW JONES

Healing

But Peter said, 'I have no silver or gold, but what I have I give you; in the name of Jesus Christ of Nazareth, stand up and walk.' And he took him by the right hand and raised him up; and immediately his feet and ankles were made strong. Jumping up, he stood and began to walk, and he entered the temple with them, walking and leaping and praising God.

One of the striking realities of both the Gospels and the book of Acts is the high number of people who have physical or mental illnesses (described as unclean spirits). As Jesus and his disciples encountered these people, he and they must have been deeply affected by them. Meeting those who were disfigured by suffering probably left a mark on Jesus' humanity and that of his disciples, eliciting their compassion and attentiveness to those in need. Healing as performed by Jesus and some of the other disciples always carries a significant theological dimension as they portray the 'gospel in action' and are always moments in which the kingdom of God is revealed.

In this passage from Acts, it is Peter who performs the act of healing and the account follows the usual healing pattern described in the Gospels—namely, the exposition of the illness (Acts 3:1–5), the healer's words and gestures (vv. 6–7), the demonstration of the cure (v. 8) and the effect on the bystanders (vv. 9–10). In verses 6–8, Peter heals the lame man by using the name of Christ. 'Name' and 'power' are parallel concepts (this is also to be seen in Acts 4:7) and Peter's invocation of the name of Jesus empowers him to perform the act of healing. This is in no way a magical performance but the medium through which the risen and ascended Christ continues his ministry of healing that was granted as a result of confession of faith in him (see also Acts 3:16 and 4:10).

We may not be great healers, but we can contribute to the healing of others in simple and faithful ways, thus enabling Jesus' ministry to continue.

ANDREW JONES

Gratitude and humility

You have turned my mourning into dancing; you have taken off my sackcloth and clothed me with joy, so that my soul may praise you and not be silent. O Lord my God, I will give thanks to you for ever.

There was a tradition that an Israelite who had come close to death but had survived would make a pilgrimage to the temple to offer a sacrifice of thanksgiving. During such a visit, a temple official—possibly a Levite—would offer to sing a thanksgiving hymn. Psalm 30 is possibly one such hymn, expressing the intention to praise God (v. 2) and explain the reasons for such praising (vv. 2–4, 7–12).

The whole psalm is addressed to God apart from verses 5–6, which address the bystanders, who are invited to join in praising God, not so much for what God actually did to the healed person but, rather, for what God is typically like and typically does for those who are in need or trouble. Interestingly, early Christians prayed this psalm to express the experience of Jesus in his sufferings and resurrection. By doing so, the actual thanksgiving for God's protection becomes a confession of the restoration of the dead Christ to new life. Indeed, the death of Christ and his resurrection to new life is the very matrix of all our experiences as Christians. In my own ministry as a priest, I come across many people who find this psalm both comforting and 'useful' in their prayer lives. Sometimes they use it for themselves and on other occasions use it on behalf of others. Christians engaged in healthcare, pastoral ministry of various kinds, counselling and education will witness transformations and restorations in people's lives. This psalm is for those who witness such changes and for those who have themselves been restored 'to life'. It is the same God who once brought recovery to that Israelite who journeyed to the temple to praise God who still gives life, hope and healing and to whom glory and praise is given.

Let's pause today to recognise in our own lives how God has delivered us from any kind of 'death' and how he has brought us home.

ANDREW JONES

Miracles

Jesus said, 'Take away the stone.'... When he had said this, he cried with a loud voice, 'Lazarus, come out!' The dead man came out, his hands and feet bound with strips of cloth, and his face wrapped in a cloth. Jesus said to them, 'Unbind him, and let him go.'

As we continue to explore in general terms the 'gifts of the Spirit' as listed by Paul in 1 Corinthians 12, the overlap between them is quite striking. This can be seen especially as we move from 'healing' to 'miracles'. Over the years, the latter gift has been defined in many and varied ways, but I want to explore the gift of miracles or, as some translate the word, 'deeds of power' as that which is effective against any obstacle or constraint because it is validated by God as opposed to human aspirations, which may, of course, fail.

On the whole, for Paul, miracles are, I think, the spiritual powers in heaven operating to castigate the power of sin, law and death. It is the process by which individuals receive, through the Spirit, liberation from their dominion and this is the heritage of all Christian believers, not simply a gift for a few. There is the sense of collectiveness about this gift, but it is true to say that only some are given the actual gift so as to show the 'gospel in action', but always for the good of all.

The word that I find useful to explain this overlap between the gifts of the Spirit is 'life'—Christ came to give life in all its abundance. The account of the healing of Lazarus epitomises Christ's offering of life. The healing of the blind man in John 9 demonstrated Jesus as the 'light' of the world and, now, in the raising of Lazarus, Jesus is its life—its heart. One of the interesting aspects of this particular miracle is that it is a shared experience. It is not Jesus who moves away the stone, it is not Jesus who unbinds Lazarus and it is not Jesus who lets him go; it is the gathered people who do these things, but always at Jesus' invitation.

Jesus promised us that he had come to give us life and, further, invited us to live life in all its abundance. Truly taking up that invitation is surely the biggest miracle of all.

ANDREW JONES

The prayer of Jonah

Then Jonah prayed to the Lord his God from the belly of the fish, say-ing, 'I called to the Lord out of my distress, and he answered me; out of the belly of Sheol I cried, and you heard my voice… But I with the voice of thanksgiving will sacrifice to you; what I have vowed I will pay. Deliverance belongs to the Lord!'

There is an irony about the book of Jonah because it is the story of a prophet who spent time and energy trying to disobey God. He had been told by God to go to Nineveh, Assyria's capital city and the enemy of Israel, but Jonah kept refusing to go because he was afraid of appearing foolish as he did not trust that God would carry out his promise to defeat the enemies of Israel. It appears that his view of God was pretty low and he regarded God as a ridiculous 'softie', con-stantly making a fool of himself by being forgiving. Jonah was keen to distance himself from what he believed to be God's constant soft approach to sinners. I guess Jonah felt that there was no real point going to Nineveh and talking about God's judgement only to dis-cover later that God would end up being a coward and forgiving the Assyrians—that would make Jonah appear a real fool! So, he declined the invitation and suggested that God look elsewhere for a more suitable advocate.

God's loving, forgiving and accepting ways vexed and disheart-ened Jonah, but Jonah didn't decline simply to save face. It was more to do with his distorted view of justice. Jonah believed that God should do that which is just and get on with severely punishing the wicked, otherwise there would be no hope of anyone actually taking God seriously. The Book of Jonah is not really about an unhappy, discontented young prophet, but about God. Jonah's prayer shows that he did ultimately recognise his own dependence on God.

Imagine what could happen if we began thinking less in terms of justice and rights and more in terms of covenant and forgiveness. Our God is a God of utter forgiveness. Who are we, then, to constantly demand harsh 'justice' for others?

ANDREW JONES

Prophecy

'Truly I tell you, many prophets and righteous people longed to see what you see, but did not see it, and to hear what you hear, but did not hear it.'

One of the exercises I enjoy when wrestling with some of the Bible's mysteries is trying to spot the ways in which the New Testament is foreshadowed in the Old Testament and the Old Testament fulfilled in the New. It is an exciting and worthwhile exercise and one that assures us of scriptural unity and continuity. By doing this, connections are made and 'pennies drop'! For example, John the Baptist's proclamation of Jesus as 'the Lamb of God' (John 1:29) fulfils and completes the account of the Passover in Exodus 12, where the blood of the lamb is put on the doorposts and lintels of the homes of God's chosen, and, in turn, Exodus 15 is a foreshadowing of John 1:2.

This is particularly obvious with 'prophecy'—the prophets' constant promise that the Messiah will eventually come—the fulfilment of those promises and prophecies being Jesus Christ. So it is that, here, we read of what could only have been anticipated with longing by the people of the Old Testament and can be enjoyed fully by the followers of Jesus—their dreams and visions have become reality.

Paul's use of 'prophecy' as one of the gifts of the Spirit combines his pastoral insight and the needs of people, communities and situations, such as existed in Corinth, with the ability to address these needs with a God-given utterance. That word, in turn, leads to challenge or comfort or judgement or consolation, so as to build up the community he is addressing. Whereas prophecy in the Old Testament is clearly a gift given to a specific office, and those who hold such office tend to stick to certain modes of ecstatic utterance, in the New Testament I am less sure that it is given to certain individuals. As a spiritual gift, it carries the function of announcing and proclaiming the gospel of Jesus Christ and doing so as communities—as churches.

Prophecy is not foretelling but, rather, forth-telling—the offer of light for the present moment.

ANDREW JONES

Elijah takes on the prophets of Baal

So Ahab sent to all the Israelites, and assembled the prophets at Mount Carmel. Elijah then came near to all the people, and said, 'How long will you go limping with two different opinions? If the Lord is God, follow him; but if Baal, then follow him.' The people did not answer him a word.

It is clear from Paul's references to prophecy that prophetic utterances come from the Holy Spirit, but mistakes can be made and, as believers are still fallible humans, claims to prophecy must be weighed and tested—hence the gift of discernment.

The story of Elijah the Tishbite develops two major themes in 1 Kings: opposition between different prophetic gifts and the portrayal of prophetic life. On the whole, in the Old Testament, the prophets are known primarily because of their utterances, often introduced by the words, 'Thus says the Lord'. Over several generations, such utterances were treasured, remembered and collated by other members of various communities. Many of the prophets emerged as highly imaginative characters and shared certain characteristics of speech. There were three main types of ministry: a ministry of judgement that indicted Israel for disobedience to God's commands and sentenced its people to punishments in line with sanctions relating to the covenant; a ministry that summoned Israel to repent and return to obedience to the covenant; and a ministry that promised new gifts of well-being that God would give.

The effect of this was to assert that all of life was lived in God's presence and must align with God's purposes. Prophecy in this sense is as important today as it ever was, but I wonder if the days of the angry prophets, such as Elijah, are over? Is God calling for something prophetically new? Probably I would want to say 'yes' to both those questions. We need our own Christian communities to become prophetic.

This will only happen when our Christian communities remain true to their prophetic heart—only then can they develop the transformative capacity that our fragmented world so desperately needs.

ANDREW JONES

Discernment

Beloved, do not believe every spirit, but test the spirits to see whether they are from God; for many false prophets have gone out into the world. By this you know the Spirit of God: every spirit that confesses that Jesus Christ has come in the flesh is from God.

For Paul, there was clearly a distinction between the divine and the human spirit and he encourages his readers to discern the genuine transcendent activity of the Spirit from merely human attempts to mimic it. This process includes a pastoral discernment of the varied ways in which the Spirit of God is working, in such a way as to distinguish various consequences. Essentially, the criterion for assessing the difference between both spirits is to search for the one that promotes and bears witness to Jesus Christ in the public domain.

Similarly, for John, there is a duality of spirits, but, in John's writing, there is a slight difference of interpretation. For him, the opposition is between the spirit of truth and the spirit of error and it reveals a sharp division between those who 'know' God and hear his true witnesses and the 'world' under Satan, which only hears what belongs to it (John 15: 19–21). Both Paul and John agree, however, that the Spirit of truth (John) and the divine Spirit (Paul) is sent to bear witness to Jesus in the Christian community and the world (John 15:27).

One of the challenges this raises is that of discerning the Spirit of truth within our own personal lives. To do so, each of us is required to discover an attentiveness and inner vigilance—the ability to concentrate and listen so as to discover what is essential in our lives. Personal discernment also means recognising our own limitations and what is incomplete about our lives. Discerning our personal 'poverty' and discerning the activity of God deep within us becomes an experience of God's grace, mercy, forgiveness and love.

Lord, help us today not to separate these two parts of our spiritual journey—knowing ourselves and knowing God. Give us the true gift of discernment.

ANDREW JONES

Listen, discern and enter in

But this is the covenant that I will make with the house of Israel after those days, says the Lord: I will put my law within them, and I will write it on their hearts; and I will be their God, and they shall be my people.

Discerning the Spirit of truth enables us to take further steps towards either renewing our covenant with God or establishing one for the first time. The notion of a covenant is one of the most consistent themes running right through the Old Testament—it was the means by which human beings were invited by God to enter into a relationship with him.

The biblical writers stress the fundamental thrust of the implications of being a covenanted people—living under the sovereignty of God and his mercy—but something different occurs in the book of Jeremiah. He offers a new perspective on the covenant relationship. For him, it is precisely because the covenant is both a source of obligation and a blessing that God shows faithfulness to his people. Jeremiah talks in terms of a new covenant (31:31–34)—one that is made between God and individuals, as opposed to a whole nation. Jeremiah brings the experience of covenant down to a much more personal level—more so than the other prophets—and seems to be suggesting that, under the new covenant, the individual is called to listen carefully for God's invitation, discern the Spirit of truth and respond by saying 'Yes'.

All of that was way back in the days of the prophets, but things have not changed and there is a ring of contemporary truth in Jeremiah's message about it being a personal relationship. We, too, are invited to listen, discern and say 'Yes', but where will that 'Yes' take us today? Hopefully, it will encourage us to proclaim with joy the good news of the kingdom of God, strengthen us to respond lovingly to the needs of others, inspire us to do all that is necessary to transform injustices and lead us to defend the natural world created by God.

May we find space to listen, discern and say 'Yes' to God's whisper.

ANDREW JONES

Prayer and tongues

I thank God that I speak in tongues more than all of you; nevertheless, in church I would rather speak five words with my mind, in order to instruct others also, than ten thousand words in a tongue.

On the whole, when Paul discusses the spiritual gift of praying in tongues, he is talking about a form of inspired prayer and praise, identified as praying or singing in the Spirit (1 Corinthians 14:15). As he addresses the Corinthians here, he distinguishes between prophecy and tongues. Prophecy is primarily a form of speech that emanates from God and is addressed to the community or to individuals within a particular Christian community. Tongues, however, is a form of prayer addressed by individuals within the community to God. In his first letter to the Corinthians, Paul is criticising the people for attaching undue importance to this gift. It seems that they used this mysterious form of unintelligible sound as a sign that they were 'spiritual', with an enhanced social position in the community. Paul regarded it as being individualistic and questioned its use in a community setting (contrasting it to the gift of prophecy). In verses 13–19, however, he concedes that tongues can make a contribution to the community, if they can be interpreted and made intelligible.

For Paul, worship and prayer are intelligible corporate experiences, the goal of which is not so much a personal spiritual injection but, rather, a building up of the body of Christ, whereby all of the gathered faithful members are able to respond with the word 'Amen' (v. 16), signifying both understanding and agreement.

'Amen' is an interesting word. It not only signifies an endorsement of what has been heard but is also a sign that the one who utters the word is prepared to nail his or her colours to the mast. Elsewhere, Paul uses the word in the context of his own commitment to put into action what he has spoken in words (2 Corinthians 1:15–22). This reflects God's faithful promise to remain true to what he has spoken (2 Corinthians 1:18, 20).

Each time we say 'Amen', let's be committed to what we are endorsing.

ANDREW JONES

An interactive conversation

'Deliver me, please, from the hand of my brother, from the hand of Esau, for I am afraid of him; he may come and kill us all, the mothers with the children. Yet you have said, "I will surely do you good, and make your offspring as the sand of the sea, which cannot be counted because of their number."'

Prayer in the Old Testament is always an interactive conversation—a drama, a dialogue—in which both parties have a role to play. The chief hallmark of these prayers is the naming of God as the one who has actively intervened on behalf of the nation and pledged an abiding loyalty to his people. In some of the prayers the nation speaks as a whole (Psalm 107:6) and at other times they are uttered by individuals (Genesis 18:22–32; Exodus 32:11–14; 2 Samuel 7:18–29). On each occasion, however, the prayers carry the reality of covenant and the fact that both parties have sworn allegiance to each other. When the covenant is good, the prayers express praise, trustful intimacy and confidence (Psalm 40), but when the covenant is in disarray, the prayers seek to reach across the breach in repentance and regret (Psalm 51). The interactive conversations experienced between God and his people are open to every issue that may occur in human life, always with the conviction that they are relevant to and adequate for every circumstance.

The rich array of things prayed for indicates that the Israel of the Old Testament was a deeply prayerful people. Three aspects of this praying nation stand out as being of particular importance. First, their prayers are real addresses to a real partner (God) in anticipation of a real response (Psalm 107). Second, their prayers are not 'mechanical', as if God's response is automatic (Psalm 88). Third, their prayers demonstrate a trustful theological innocence (1 Samuel 1—2).

Before he meets Esau, Jacob's prayer has a clear structure: he addresses God by name, expresses self-deprecation, makes a sincere petition, describes his distress, gives the motivation for God to intervene and even reminds God of his promise. Not a bad pattern for us to follow.

ANDREW JONES

1 John: a love letter

'This is the message we have heard from him and proclaim to you, that God is light and in him there is no darkness at all' (1 John 1:5).

How wonderful it must have been to have received such joyous, confident statements in those difficult, challenging times of the early Christian era. Surrounded by pagans, facing the issues that beset groups of people when they try to change their lives and live together in peace and community, John's first letter would have shone with the light of love that he wrote about, illuminating the darkness of struggle and fear.

It is probable that the author of this letter is the same man who wrote the Gospel, the disciple John, trying to encourage the disciples in Asia Minor who were in his special care. This letter is filled with love—God's love for us and, by natural progression, our own love for God and each other. It is written by the disciple Jesus perhaps loved best—the one he called 'beloved', the only disciple at the crucifixion, the one who was charged with the care of Jesus' mother, the first to believe in the resurrection. At the end of his life, reflecting on all he had said and done in Jesus' name, John sat down to write his Gospel and his love letters.

What a transformation from the rough fisherman Jesus first met! How different from the hot-tempered character who, together with his brother James, was known as the 'son of thunder' (Mark 3:17). How changed from the angry man who offered to rain fire on the unbelievers of Samaria (Luke 9:51–55)!

John's transformation is neither sudden nor dramatic. Gradually, as the story of Jesus unfolds, he changes and develops until, with maturity and reflection, he arrives at a love-filled, light-soaked life and his first concern is to share it with others.

In John's first letter, we have a glimpse of the changes that Christ can make in the hearts and minds and lives of those who try to walk in his paths. Let us pray for the grace to allow him to make those changes in us also.

SALLY WELCH

And did those feet...?

We declare to you what was from the beginning, what we have heard, what we have seen with our eyes, what we have looked at and touched with our hands, concerning the word of life.

One of the reasons most frequently given by Christians for visiting the Holy Land is that they want to see the places they have read about in the New Testament. Hundreds of thousands of believers travel each year to Israel to sail on a boat on the Sea of Galilee, gaze at the site of the nativity in Bethlehem and kneel, with fellow Christians, in the garden of Gethsemane. To be physically present in those same places that the historical Jesus visited is a very powerful experience and can strengthen faith and be an aid to prayer.

For the readers of John's letters, just as for many of us, such travel was not possible, but they had, instead, something even more powerful—a witness. They had the words of one who had not only visited the towns and villages of Jesus' healing and teaching but also been with him when those wonderful, miraculous events had occurred. Believe what is written in this letter, writes John, because its author saw Jesus, walked with him, shared his physical life and knows it to be true.

John shares his witness, his experience of the Son of God, the Word from God and of God, whose saving mission was so much more than healings or encouraging stories to help us live our lives in a better way. The Word of life had come to all people to bring life as it is meant to be, its wonderful potential fully realised as a gift to all who asked. 'Life itself had come to life, had taken the form of a human being, coming into the present from God's future' (Tom Wright, *Early Christian Letters for Everyone*, SPCK, 2011).

Loving Father, we thank you for the witness of those who have experienced Jesus' life-giving love in their lives. Give us the grace to share our own experience of that love, through our words and actions, that others too may have life.

SALLY WELCH

You also may have fellowship

We declare to you what we have seen and heard so you also may have fellowship with us; and truly our fellowship is with the Father and with his Son Jesus Christ. We are writing these things so that our joy may be complete.

One of my first impulses when I have read a book I particularly enjoyed or seen a film that I found moving or interesting is to tell my friends about it, encouraging them to read or watch so that they too may experience the same emotions or insights. If the book or film is outstanding, I will often go so far as to lend or buy the book or DVD for them to make sure they have access to the experience.

It is clear from this passage that, similarly, John's driving impulse is to be a witness to the wonderful gift of life he has received so that others may share in it, but for much more compelling benefits than those I have gained from a book or a film. John is impelled to share this new life with everyone so that they too will believe and be brought into fellowship with other believers. The word he uses for 'fellowship' is the word that is used in ancient Greek for especially close and intimate relationships. It is a word particularly employed when describing the marriage bond, but is also used for other mutually dependent, loving and sharing relationships. It is this kind of relationship that we are being invited to be a part of, but not just with other believers, for our fellowship is with God the Father and God the Son, sharing the inner reality of life in all its fullness and joy. We are invited to live in a spiritual unity that is rooted in the gospel, articulated through our words and actions. The results of this unity, we are promised, will be joyful and fulfilling as we grow and deepen our relationship with God and our fellow human beings, through Christ.

Lord, let me hear your word of life and, having heard it,
share it with others so that all may live in unity and
fellowship with each other and with you.

SALLY WELCH

If we say that we have no sin...

If we say that we have no sin, we deceive ourselves, and the truth is not in us. If we confess our sins, he who is faithful and just will forgive us our sins and cleanse us from all unrighteousness.

I recently visited someone who was in the midst of moving house—all the furniture had been removed and he was going round each room checking that nothing had been left behind. We remarked that when the house was full of furniture and ornaments and people, it had looked very tidy and well kept. Now that it was empty, however, all the little knocks and scratches of everyday life were evident on the walls and paintwork and the house looked scruffy, in need of a new coat of paint.

It can be easy to think that because we commit no major errors, say nothing outrageously mean or carry out no cruel actions, we are relatively free from sin. We do not realise, however, that our lives are full of the things of the world—its opinions, its values, its judgements. Just like furniture in the house, these things obstruct our view of our sins and we cannot see ourselves clearly for who we are. In the light of Christ and his saving sacrifice, however, all our faults and unkindnesses are revealed and we learn the true extent of our sins. God has a way through our sins—the way of forgiveness, freely offered. When we acknowledge our sins, we open the path to this forgiveness, a path created by Christ, who has already been punished for them on our behalf. Were we to seek justice, we would be lost, but the debt has already been paid for us. We deserve God's judgement; because of Christ, we receive his mercy.

Take time to reflect carefully on your words and actions at the end of this day. How have you fallen short of expressing God's love? Clear your soul of the world's judgements and allow the light of Christ to shine on its darkest corners, bringing to light your smallest sins. Then allow yourself to feel the mercy and grace of God's forgiveness as it fills your heart.

SALLY WELCH

I abide in him

By this we may be sure that we are in him: whoever says, 'I abide in him' ought to walk just as he walked.

Moving house, however local that move might be, opens the door to change. The old dwelling is left behind and all the furniture and other belongings are given new positions. Then the process of truly settling in to this new home begins. We discover how things work, the particular quirks of the heating system, the delights of the surroundings. We may go further afield, exploring, meeting our neighbours and doing various activities that mean we will feel settled and established in our new home.

Following Jesus means changing our whole lives—or, rather, allowing ourselves to be totally transformed by him. We must take up new habits, get used to new ways of life, adopt new ways of thinking and speaking and act in a different way from how we did formerly. This can be challenging work, with not a little effort and sometimes quite a lot of regret for those easier days when our words and actions had only to conform to the ways of the world, rather than the demanding way of love in which Jesus leads us. We will make mistakes, we will sin, for this is an inevitable part of human nature, but our attitude towards sin will be changed and the promise of forgiveness for sin repented will never be taken from us. Learning to abide in Christ, to cease our aimless seeking after each new thrill and possession, and to accept the demands of love, can be difficult, but the rewards are eternal. Our relationships with God and neighbour will change and develop in depth and beauty, our forgiven selves will grow to meet the challenges of this earthly life and always, as we strive to 'walk just as he walked' (v. 6), there will be the knowledge that we do not walk alone.

Henry Lyte's famous hymn 'Abide with me', based on Jesus' encounter with the disciples on the road to Emmaus (Luke 24:13–35), contains the line 'come not to sojourn but abide with me'. Let this be our prayer as we seek to dwell with Christ and in Christ.

SALLY WELCH

The world and its desire

Do not love the world or the things in the world. The love of the Father is not in those who love the world; for all that is in the world—the desire of the flesh, the desire of the eyes, the pride in riches—comes not from the Father but from the world. And the world and its desire are passing away, but those who do the will of God live for ever.

If we abide in Christ, if we dwell in him and allow his love to take root in our hearts and souls, there will be no room for the earthly desires that so corrupt and tarnish our world.

John warns his readers that greed and acquisitiveness in any area, whether it be in human relationships or material goods, can harm our well-being and distract us from seeking after God and his love. Indeed, he warns that those who cling too tightly to the things of the world will not leave any energy or time for the things of God as our minds will become confused and filled with unimportant things and we will cease our quest for intimacy with God in Christ. This does not mean, however, that we should renounce our enjoyment of the good things of God's creation. Not only may we take pleasure in food and drink, the natural world and human companionship but it is also right that we should do so as these were created by God for our enjoyment and pleasure. We must use God's gifts, so freely and generously given, as a way of deepening our relationship with him and with our neighbour—they are a means to an end rather than an end in themselves. John warns us not to chase after ephemeral attractions, which will wither and fade, but, rather, focus on the coming kingdom and those joys that will last forever.

Teach us, O Lord, not to chase after the temporary butterflies of this world, which seek to distract us from our true goal of life in Christ. Rather, show us how to rejoice in your creation, finding in it the evidence of your great love for us.

SALLY WELCH

See what love!

See what love the Father has given us, that we should be called children of God; and that is what we are.

During my years as a parish priest, I have spent many hours leading toddler services. These usually begin with parents, carers and children gathering together in a group. An opening song is followed by a Bible story, usually told with the aid of props, such as knitted figures or soft toys. A simple prayer is then followed by more songs before the group scatters for coffee, biscuits and conversation, while the children play in the church. This time together is one for closeness and calm, as far as possible, with the children sitting on laps and being held by those who love them, while they hear the stories of a God who loved them first and loves them best.

Those of us who experienced similarly loving and happy relationships in childhood and beyond should never cease to be grateful for that first experience of love, which shapes our future encounters. Not all children are fortunate enough to experience the sort of love that I see weekly demonstrated in the groups I work with. Many, both in our country and throughout the world, grow into adulthood with no knowledge of the self-sacrificing tenderness that should be theirs by right but has been withheld from them. There is, however, one whose love is greater than that of earthly parents, completely self-giving and never falters or fails. The love of God the Father, expressed through his gift to us of God the Son, dwelling within us in the Holy Spirit, is perfect and permanent. It heals the wounds inflicted on us by the events of the world and makes us whole. We are adopted through love, chosen in love, to be God's children and can rest safely in the knowledge of that love, just as a small baby may rest in a mother's arms, cradled in love.

---

*What is it like to rest in the arms of God? How safe we can feel
in the knowledge of his protecting, shielding love!*

SALLY WELCH

God's children now

Beloved, we are God's children now; what we will be has not yet been revealed. What we do know is this: when he is revealed, we will be like him, for we will see him as he is.

In the mid-17th century, a young Frenchman, Nicholas Herman, joined a monastery. He took the name Brother Lawrence and was set to work in the kitchen. There, for the most part, he remained, scrubbing dishes, peeling vegetables and serving meals. This might seem a very inglorious way to spend a life, but it was while he did these chores that Brother Lawrence developed a powerful and joyful spirituality of work and life. Brother Lawrence's approach was simple: people make a big thing out of trying to encounter God, but, 'Is it not quicker and easier just to do our common business wholly for the love of him?' In this way, even the humblest task becomes an act of worship and gains great value through that: 'It is enough for me to pick up but a straw from the ground for the love of God.'

In the focused discipline of bringing God's presence to mind continually throughout the day will be found the joyful rewards of taking whatever opportunity we can to dedicate our actions to God. We will experience a changed attitude to the world, the people around us and ourselves as we appreciate the gift of love that is in God, in the immediate moment.

'We are God's children now', writes John (v. 2). We do not have to wait for God's love or earn the right to be called his children; all this is ours already. Our task is simply to rejoice in that love and share it so that our full potential as children of God can be realised. Ours is not to fret about the future, but, instead, to celebrate the miracle of the incarnate God, the miracle of God's compassionate awareness and loving acceptance poured into each moment, enfolding us in a love that will hold us securely—as it always has done and will continue to do, into eternity.

Loving Father, help me to find your love in every moment of my life.

SALLY WELCH

And again

For this is the message you have heard from the beginning, that we
should love one another.

If the Psalter in the Book of Common Prayer is followed faithfully,
with the set Psalms being read or chanted each day, all 150 Psalms
are read during the course of just one month. In a cathedral setting,
where the choir will chant the Psalms at Evensong each evening, this
means that, in the course of a year, they are heard again and again.
Phrases settle deep into the consciousness, bubbling up in conversations, springing to mind in moments of crisis, resonating clearly
when they are heard in different contexts. This is particularly so in
the case of the young choristers, whose impressionable minds are
saturated with the wisdom and courage of those who engaged so
completely with their faith many centuries ago. Boys and girls can be
heard echoing phrases as they run in the playground, singing chants
in the lunch queue, at one with the minds of the long-dead writers
of such memorable lines. These words become part of who they are,
the sentiments absorbed into their psyches to remain there for ever.

The constant repetition of John's main message in his letters has
the same aim, its powerful simplicity, plain but vital, being urged on
us again and again. Love God and love your neighbour, we are told
repeatedly, in the hope that this teaching will become part of our
subconscious, part of the very depth of who we are, influencing
every aspect of our lives.

Loving God and neighbour is foundational to all Christianity. If
God is love, then we cannot have a relationship with God without
being transformed ourselves into people of love. If we become such
people, then it is only logical that the love we have for God, through
God, given by God, should flow out from us towards other people.
Thus, we hear it, again and again, throughout this short book, as John
tries urgently to share his message with all those who might listen.

---

*'How precious is your unfailing love, O God! All humanity finds shelter
in the shadow of your wings' (Psalm 36:7).*

SALLY WELCH

In truth and action

How does God's love abide in anyone who has the world's goods and sees a brother or sister in need and yet refuses help? Little children, let us love, not in word or speech, but in truth and action.

There is always a danger—if we are passionately interested in something, but a little bit apprehensive about our ability to join in—that we spend so much time reading, thinking and learning about an activity, there is no time left actually to engage with it on a personal, physical level.

John is very clear that this must not happen with our faith. It is not enough just to proclaim about love and meet in groups to discuss its qualities and effects. It is not enough even to talk about how deeds of love might best be carried out, although a certain amount of talking and discussion is undeniably useful. A Christian attitude of love must spill out into our actions—there must always be a practical application of those things we have heard, learned and discussed. Faith becomes truly alive in the action. The impulse to do good, share those things we have, come to the aid of a friend, neighbour or stranger, whether it is by offering practical help or simply listening, is the overspill from a heart that is filled with love. Loving deeds are the proof that the heart itself is filled with the love of God, for God's love cannot abide in those who refuse help to another.

I am reminded of the story of David's anointing (1 Samuel 16), where Samuel sees all but one of Jesse's sons rejected, despite their outward suitability for the role of king. God, though, has other criteria: 'Do not look on his appearance or on the height of his stature because I have rejected him; for the Lord does not see as mortals see; they look on the outward appearance, but the Lord looks on the heart' (1 Samuel 16:6–7).

Loving God, help us to share the love we have received from you in our actions as well as our words.

SALLY WELCH

God will reassure our hearts

And by this we will know that we are from the truth and will reassure our hearts before him whenever our hearts condemn us; for God is greater than our hearts, and he knows everything.

When I was working as a parish priest, I met a wonderful couple, generous and kind, whose hospitality formed part of the bedrock of the church's mission in that town. They would come regularly to church, but the man would never come to the Communion rail, not even for a blessing. When I asked him about this, he replied that he had fought in World War II and done things so terrible that not even God could forgive him.

During the course of many conversations with him and with great support from his wife and friends, he came to believe that no sin was beyond God's saving power and he too could be forgiven. He was not the only person who wept when finally he received Communion for the first time in 50 years.

We know how unworthy we are, how often we fail to say or do those things we should, how many of our actions are coloured by sin, and we can be tormented by this knowledge. Many times, indeed, our hearts condemn us. John does not belittle these feelings of guilt and self-condemnation—he takes them very seriously. He demonstrates, however, lovingly, that this does not put us outside God's loving forgiveness. Our faults are not minimised or dismissed—God is completely aware of how many there are and how far we are from living perfect lives—but we can be reassured by the knowledge that we abide in God's love and can confess freely to all our sins, confident in his grace and secure in his love. Nothing is beyond God's power of forgiveness; nothing is beyond his mercy.

Father of all, forgive us when we believe our sins put us beyond your power to save. Let the knowledge of your love reassure our hearts when they condemn us and help us to put our faith in your loving redemption.

SALLY WELCH

Believe and love

And this is his commandment, that we should believe in the name of his Son Jesus Christ and love one another, just as he has commanded us. All who obey his commandments abide in him and he abides in them.

Christianity is a wonderful, complex thing. It often seems to me that, however much studying I do, however deeply I venture into the waters of practical theology or Bible studies or any one of a hundred other subjects connected with Christianity, there will always be more to discover, more to learn, more information that helps to throw some light on the subject. Yet, at its heart, Christianity is incredibly simple. It is this very simplicity that makes it so compelling.

All we need to do, John tells us here, as he has told us many times before, is to believe and to love. We must believe, or at least struggle to believe, that the God who created the universe revealed himself in his Word, through which the world itself was made. The Word came down and dwelt with us, teaching us how to live in the light of God. In order that we might continue in this light, the Word then died for us, taking all our sins on himself. The only possible response to this revelation of love is to love in return, to love not only God, the originator of love, but, through Christ, also love each other.

Biblical commentaries state that the verb used in this passage for 'love' is in the present tense. John uses this to remind us that this love is a continual state. God has always loved us and always will, Christ is always redeeming us from our sins and our response should be a constant outpouring of love towards him and towards those who also share that love. In today's passage, that powerful word 'abide' occurs once more. We can be rooted, settled, in love and, in that confident abiding, reach out to others.

Loving God, give me the grace to abide in your love and, in that abiding, become part of the endless love that flows out into the world.

SALLY WELCH

In this is love

God's love was revealed among us in this way: God sent his only Son into the world so that we might live through him. In this is love, not that we loved God but that he loved us and sent his Son to be the atoning sacrifice for our sins.

On Good Friday, in a short service for families and young children, we aim to involve the community in the story of the final hours of Jesus' life. We adopt a holistic approach—people are invited to taste the bread of the Last Supper, smell the flowers that might have grown in Gethsemane, hear the sounds of soldiers approaching to arrest Jesus. In this way, the full impact of Jesus' suffering is made clearer to us. We end the story looking at a large crucifix that hangs above the steps to the chancel and everyone is invited to leave an offering at the foot of the cross—a paper heart, a footprint, a pipe-cleaner cross. For a short time, there is a strange silence, heavy with emotion. Then the mood breaks and hot cross buns and drinks are served and the atmosphere returns almost to normal, but there remains a lingering feeling of unfinished business, of waiting, a story half told. Not until Easter Sunday will the glorious conclusion be reached. Until then, the community pauses and reflects.

John, too, invites us to pause at the foot of the cross and spend just a short time there, contemplating the true nature of God's love. It is here, in this breathless pause, while the whole of creation waits for the work of God to be completed, that we may begin to have just an idea of the power of love. It is here, too, that our response to God's love is born, as surely one who loves us so much should be loved in return! Surely such love is so powerful that it can change the world! Surely we, too, can play our parts in this transforming, liberating, all-embracing love.

O dearly, dearly has he loved, and we must love him too,
And trust in his redeeming love and try his works to do.

Mrs C.F. Alexander (1818–1895)

SALLY WELCH

God is love

God is love, and those who abide in love abide in God, and God abides
in them.

Over the years, I have taken many marriage services. Some have been
small, intimate affairs, with no more than a handful of guests and a
trip to the pub afterwards, and others have dazzled me with their
grandeur and the number of flower arrangements it is possible to fit
into one church. Whatever they are like, however, I begin each one
with this wonderful sentence from John's letter. It is my declaration
that whatever the financial or physical circumstances of the marriage, the personal reservations members of the congregation may
hold about its success in the future and doubts the individuals may
privately hold about the existence of God, the lives of this couple
have begun in love and, because they have begun in love, they have
begun with God. God is present with them and will remain with
them while they negotiate the tricky pathway of their journey
through life. God is present with them and, should they ask, will give
them the strength, courage and grace to grow in understanding and
increase in love for each other.

This sentence of John's is vitally important for us and our understanding of what it is to be a Christian. It is one simple declaration
about the nature of love and the role God plays in that love, setting
each one of us free to love everyone we encounter in our lives. The
role of judging who is or is not worthy to be loved is not ours, nor is
the option of not loving, because we cannot love God without loving
each other. All we must do is nurture the gift of love that we have
been given through God and share it with those whom we meet,
whoever they are, wherever we meet them. Such is the strength and
power of God's love that we can rest secure that God will do the rest.

---

*Loving Father, creator of all things, help us to believe that all
those who live in love live in God. Help us to love others as you
love us, that we may continue to abide in you, and you in us.*

SALLY WELCH

The boldness we have in him

I write these things to you who believe in the name of the Son of God,
so that you may know that you have eternal life. And this is the bold-
ness we have in him, that if we ask anything according to his will, he
hears us.

Carefully and with great attention, John has shared with his fellow
believers the fundamental elements of the Christian faith: belief and
love. These two elements form the bedrock of a Christian understanding of the world and a Christian attitude towards it. They are
mutually dependent—no one can believe without love and love is
the foundation of belief. They flow from God, who first loved human
beings, and they are returned to God by us, who have been made his
children by his love. We who believe are transformed by the love of
God and will share that love with our brothers and sisters in community, standing side by side with each other in mutual support and
understanding. We need fear nothing any longer because 'perfect
love casts out fear' (1 John 4:18) and we are assured that, because of
that love, we will gain eternal life.

All this has been given to us by the one who sent his only son as
an atoning sacrifice, so that our sins should no longer come between
us and the love we need. As a final promise, John reassures us that if
we ask anything in accordance with God's will, it will be given to us,
because God hears all who pray in faith. We are given the grace to
'stand at the place where heaven and earth meet and are encouraged
to draw down the blessings of heaven into the life of earth' (Tom
Wright, *Early Christian Letters for Everyone*, SPCK, 2011).

---

*Heavenly Father, help us to recognise your gift of love, offered
to us so freely through Christ, that in turn we may increase
our gift of love to those around us and to you, 'for all things
come from you, and of your own have we given you' (1
Chronicles 29:14).*

SALLY WELCH

Fasting in the New Testament

Our attitudes to food say a great deal about our society and culture and even our personal state of mind. In our current world of obesity and poverty, excessive meat consumption and environmental degradation, this is certainly true, but we find it too at the time of the early church. As is often the case, Jesus works both with and against the grain of people's expectations of a prophet or religious leader in his attitudes to food and fasting.

I am interested in what fasting represents. These days, people might give up something they enjoy for Lent. This has become a widespread practice and I know a lot of people who have no connection with the church who give up some foodstuff or other. This is a remnant of the practice of fasting for 40 days in recognition of Jesus' time in the wilderness. Some may give the money they save as a result of their abstinence to charity. Lent itself is a time of preparation for the feast of Easter, the in-breaking of the risen Son. Early in its history, Advent, too, was a period of sobriety, reflection and fasting.

People continue to practise fasting for many other reasons, too. Many may be vegetarian, look to buy organic food or consider animal welfare. The fair trade ethos has grown in prominence in the last 20 years. Fasting can be a deliberate setting apart of oneself from everyday society or a way of pointing towards a new society. It can be about self-denial. Table fellowship is a key sign of Christian community and occurs frequently in Jesus' parables and actions. For a faith and culture where food and different recipes are an important expression of community and enjoyment, marking a festival by not eating is particularly significant. Old Testament figures practised fasts at key points in their lives, in times of mourning or preparation for God's action. Dietary requirements were important, but there was a recognition that fasting needed to go deeper and engage with social and political practices.

I am looking forward to exploring how fasting is treated in the New Testament and how it might be of relevance today.

HARRY SMART

Living in expectation

There was also a prophet, Anna the daughter of Phanuel, of the tribe of Asher. She was of a great age, having lived with her husband for seven years after her marriage, then as a widow to the age of eighty-four. She never left the temple but worshipped there with fasting and prayer night and day.

Luke's Gospel begins with the breaking in of God into people's lives. Anna appears at the presentation of Jesus to the temple. She has led a life of prayer and fasting. She would have lived on the edge of mainstream society as she was widowed in a culture in which much of a woman's identity rested on her being married. Like Simeon, she has been watching and waiting for the restoration of Israel. A sign of her prayer is that she fasts. As an observant Jew, she kept the dietary laws, which included not eating pork or shellfish, for example. Fasting can entail refraining from a midday meal or eating before daybreak and after dusk rather than not eating at all. Anna probably would not have been keeping a long-term and extreme fast.

Several years ago, I took part in a demonstration for increased cycling facilities in my home town. Several of the cyclists were quite elderly, but very aware of the need for good cycling infrastructure. As we sat eating a shared lunch, I spoke with an older woman who told me about her concern about fair trade, ethics in farming and the injustice of food waste. Her concern was inspired in part by her faith. She lived simply, buying remaindered food from the supermarkets, baking her own bread and cycling wherever she could. In her own way, she was watching and waiting for the liberation of Israel, the coming of the kingdom. Her vision of justice and a fairer life inspired others, including myself.

Anna recognised Jesus as a sign of the fulfilment of her hope. Fasting was a sign of her vision, but, rather than letting it set her apart, she went out to share her experience of fulfilment with others in need of inspiration.

What is it we hope for and how do we show that hope in our lives?

HARRY SMART

Fasting can help us know who we are

Now John wore clothing of camel's hair with a leather belt around his
waist, and his food was locusts and wild honey. Then the people of
Jerusalem and all Judea were going out to him, and all the region
along the Jordan, and they were baptised by him in the river Jordan,
confessing their sins.

There are apparently thousands of insects that are edible and John the
Baptist knew this as he went out into the desert to survive on a basic
diet of honey and locusts. He was a strange character, taking a stance
against the world of cities and towns and challenging its authorities,
both religious (the Pharisees and Saducees) and secular (the soldiers,
who he warns in Luke's Gospel not to bully or be corrupt).

John has chosen to set himself against those things that the rest of
society consider to be important and his fast is a sign of his attitude
to those priorities. The people he criticises consider themselves to be
powerful or claim a hereditary virtue that has not produced good
fruits. Is it coincidental that he is using an image connected to food?
He is rejecting the food of a self-serving, self-satisfied society and
looking to the abundant and sustaining fruit of the Holy Spirit.

John is in the tradition of those who point to an integrity expressed
through simplicity. Within that tradition are the Old Testament
prophets, some Greek philosophers and many others. Shakespeare's
King Lear (Act III, Scene 4) meets the mad Poor Tom on the heath
and recognises their common humanity and basic integrity: 'Thou
owest the worm no silk, the beast no hide, the sheep no wool, the cat
no perfume… Thou art the thing itself: unaccommodated man is no
more but such a poor, bare, forked animal as thou art.'

John's fast challenges us to re-examine those things that we consider to be essential. Jesus' ministry begins in the light of John's
preaching. Fasting and the wilderness will prove to be the defining
point for his teaching.

What are the things I can give up so that I can be more
fully the person God is calling me to be?

HARRY SMART

A Mediterranean diet

The devil said to him, 'If you are the Son of God, command this stone to become a loaf of bread.' Jesus answered him, 'It is written, "One does not live by bread alone."'

The first temptation offered to Jesus is cunning and subtle. Feeding those in need was a dear concern for him. Later he uses bread as a key symbol, in the heavenly banquet, of the kingdom of God. By rejecting the temptation he is not saying that bread is unimportant or that feeding the hungry is in vain. The temptation is only powerful because it comes close to the heart of Jesus' ministry, but food represents something deeper than simply sustenance for him—and for us.

Benedict's rule, written in AD530 for monks in a community on Monte Cassino, Italy, allows each monk a pound of bread per day. Benedict's recommendations for the monastic diet were not necessarily an expression of micromanagement. Previous monastic communities had restricted their diets more severely. Benedict recommended a surprising amount of wine per day—about half a pint, only partly explained by the fact that alcohol was safer than drinking water at that time. The consumption of meat was restricted to sick monks. Four-legged animals could not be eaten. Meat in general was not allowed for any of them on the many fast days throughout the year.

Meat, of course, was very expensive and would have been eaten much less then than it is today. This restriction was in part about living simply. Benedict's recommended diet is not punitive, but it is deliberately unostentatious. It is a diet that is less demanding of the earth's resources, has the potential to encourage greater animal welfare and can lead to sharing resources more fairly.

We are not only what we eat. What we eat, how we obtain it and relate to it are issues significant enough that they could be used as a temptation for Jesus himself, but, as the world's population passes six billion, they are ones we need to grapple with ourselves today.

What do my shopping habits say about me? Can I live
simply so that others can simply live?

HARRY SMART

Hunger in the wilderness

Jesus, full of the Holy Spirit, returned from the Jordan and was led by the Spirit in the wilderness, where for forty days he was tempted by the devil. He ate nothing at all during those days, and when they were over he was famished.

It can be seen that people in the New Testament fasted at times of transition. Paul fasts as he withdraws into himself to comprehend the calling of God. John the Baptist chooses the desert as the backdrop for his challenge to society. Jesus retreats into the wilderness to fast. Moses had fasted for 40 days before receiving the ten commandments. We are told little about that fast, however. Mark tells us very little about Jesus' temptations, but Matthew and Luke provide more details.

As though stating the obvious, we are told that by the end of the fast Jesus was famished. Those who undertake 40-day fasts (which should only be done after seeking professional medical advice) warn gravely against refusing water as part of a fast. What access Jesus had to water may have been limited. He would have been in a very weak state. It reminds me of Jesus' thirst on the cross.

I have regularly gone on walking holidays, often led by a guide. It is an excellent way to get to know an area. Sicily in the summer can be intensely hot and walking in the interior of the island was hard work. We struggled as we make our way from the shade of one gnarled olive tree to another. We had taken water with us, of course, but we were sweating so profusely that walking became painful. Perhaps I should have chosen another time to go, but I became very aware of my own physicality. As a middle-class Westerner, I have had very little experience of lack of food or drink. During those walks, I became very aware of the reality that the human body is 65 per cent water.

Fasting can remind us that we are human and we are frail. Jesus' time in the desert is profoundly relevant to us because of his frailty.

May we come to know ourselves as human beings, with our frailties and limitedness. We are God's creation!

HARRY SMART

Fasting, mourning and sorrow

Now John's disciples and the Pharisees were fasting; and people came and said to him, 'Why do John's disciples and the disciples of the Pharisees fast, but your disciples do not fast?' Jesus said to them, 'The wedding guests cannot fast while the bridegroom is with them, can they? As long as they have the bridegroom with them, they cannot fast. The days will come when the bridegroom is taken away from them, and then they will fast on that day.'

Jesus' ministry is being questioned. Jesus has been shown eating and drinking with sinners and now what he does is being compared to John's practice. Jesus evidently is not fulfilling many people's expectation that he should be practising self-denial. Some have rejected John for his asceticism, yet are implying that they should reject Jesus for being a glutton. Sometimes there is no pleasing people!

Jesus is connecting fasting with mourning and it is his own death that he is predicting. The fasting will occur at the time when he is taken away from his disciples, as it is a response to horror and loss. It is almost apocalyptic. Fasting will have its own appropriate time. What would Jesus' disciples have felt on hearing his prediction that there was hardship and denial to come? Would they have anticipated its significance? Did some of them quite like the idea of being like gluttons rather than having to practise John's abstemiousness?

'The pursuit of happiness' is identified in the USA's Declaration of Independence as one of our 'unalienable rights', along with life and liberty. We might prefer to avoid the times of mourning that will inevitably enter our lives. Fasting can express a sense of an over-turned world and be a protest against it. Fasting expresses sorrow, but, more even than feasting, it can be a sign of hope: we fast now, but the fast will be broken. There can be a rightness to sorrow, if we can trust that it will be relieved.

Where have been the times of fasting in your life? Can such times also allow new growth and development? Can God work in times of sorrow as well as in times of joy?

HARRY SMART

Strive first for the kingdom of God

'Therefore do not worry, saying "What will we eat?" or "What will we drink?" or "What will we wear?" For it is the Gentiles who strive for all these things; and indeed your heavenly Father knows that you need all these things. But strive first for the kingdom of God and his right-eousness, and all these things will be given to you as well. So do not worry about tomorrow, for tomorrow will bring worries of its own. Today's trouble is enough for today.'

Jesus eats and drinks at weddings and has spent an extended period fasting from food all together. His attitude to food is not one of dis-like or contempt. His fast in the wilderness does not mean that he generally followed a self-damaging diet. His main aim is to put food in its place—we need it, but it is not to be of primary importance or cause us to worry.

For several years I was involved in a homeless project where I worked as a mental health chaplain. At the local church, great work was done, providing sustaining food at low prices for people who had come off the streets or lived rough in tents hidden in under-growth along the river. The church brought together homeless peo-ple and others to build somewhere welcoming and safe that also taught skills and provided positive experiences. More recently, in the UK, visits to foodbanks have increased in recent years and more have been set up. People have spoken with me about the shame they felt at having to resort to charity for their food.

In this passage, Jesus is challenging us again. God's kingdom can be found where the hungry are fed, where people are prepared to share their resources and our own individual interests are held in the light of the needs of others. To eat with people who have next to noth-ing is moving and uncomfortable. It may not technically be a fast, but it encourages us to rethink our priorities and live differently.

How does my attitude to food shape my life and my relationships with others locally and further afield? Can the kingdom come into this aspect of our lives as well?

HARRY SMART

Keeping a balance

'Blessed are you who are hungry now, for you will be filled... Woe to
you who are full now, for you will be hungry.'

Here blessings are matched with woes, with the implication that 'the
times they are a-changing', as Bob Dylan sang, and soon society will
be overturned. We do tend to moderate Jesus' words and message.
While he offered hope, his words challenged the self-satisfied and
those who benefited from the poverty of those around them. They
continue to do so. The politics of food distribution and production
are complicated. Injustice in trade and consumption is deep as food
markets maintain low prices on goods from developing countries.
Fairtrade initiatives do provide hope, however.

Monastic communities were inspired to practise fasting regularly.
Modern Trappist communities are vegetarian and the diet practised
by Greek Orthodox monks has been recommended as a possible way
of losing weight and extending our lifespan. In fact, the monastic
diet combines fast and feast and promotes the consumption of plenty
of fresh vegetables and olive oil. Fewer of the reports mention the
centrality of prayer and meditation practised by the monks, though!

Key to the balance of blessing and woe that Jesus proclaims is a
warning against being self-satisfied. Being full now might be at the
expense of the poverty and hunger of others. It may prevent us from
seeing the needs of the people around us. James 1:2–4 uses the format of a speech at a dinner to convey the idea of a place where no
distinctions should be made.

In this passage, as in so many of those referring to the practice of
fasting, although it is seen to be expressive of mourning and sorrow,
of a turning away from the world or standing in opposition to it, it
always contains a sense of hope as well. There is the hope of the
broad table of God's kingdom at which all shall be welcome and at
which all shall be fulfilled in the bridegroom's company.

---

*May our times of fasting always be lifted up by anticipation of
God's heavenly banquet.*

HARRY SMART

Did I ever tell you that I...

'And whenever you fast, do not look dismal, like the hypocrites, for they disfigure their faces so as to show others that they are fasting. Truly I tell you, they have received their reward. But when you fast, put oil on your head and wash your face, so that your fasting may be seen not by others but by your Father who is in secret.'

As someone who occasionally attempts to lose weight by dieting—giving up crisps, biscuits and so on, I know the joy of telling people that I am doing so. I try to go to the gym, too—it is good to do something that contrasts with my work life, and being in the company of others spurs me on to greater efforts.

There are many diets and many religious practices. Both lead to the production of books, conferences, feature in retreats and earnest discussions among academics and practitioners. Perhaps it is a symptom of our consumerist philosophy, but we are good at creating a market out of a lifestyle or even out of a teaching that emphasises simplicity. Thus, we are encouraged to follow the latest diet, feel bad about our shape, size or appearance or buy the newest book on the most recent version of an ancient practice because, as one advert puts it, 'You're worth it'.

Jesus does not condemn fasting. He says, 'whenever you fast' rather than 'do not fast'. His Sermon on the Mount is placed shortly after his period in the desert, when fasting has been significant for him.

Jesus is interested in the motives for doing things. Without good motivation, our activities will not be successful. That motivation has to be deeper than the desire to create an external straw person without substance. It is from the living relationship between ourselves and our creator and between ourselves and others that we can begin to forge a true sense of self. Fasting can help with that, allowing us to express an inner state or helping us to concentrate on a particular point. Eating more healthily and keeping physically fit are important, too, but only if it is something I take seriously and try to commit to.

If God knows me fully, who am I trying to convince?

HARRY SMART

That is not me

'Two men went up to the temple to pray, one a Pharisee and the other a tax collector. The Pharisee, standing by himself, prayed thus, "God, I thank you that I am not like other people: thieves, rogues, adulterers, or even like this tax collector. I fast twice a week; I give a tenth of all my income." But the tax collector, standing far off, would not even look up to heaven, but was beating his breast and saying, "God, be merciful to me, a sinner!" I tell you, this man went down to his home justified rather than the other.'

This teaching is set among others about following Jesus and entering the kingdom of God. Indeed, a few verses later comes the passage about the rich man and the eye of the needle. Is Jesus suggesting that humility and a desire for forgiveness are enough and that fasting, giving tithes or even selling everything we have is empty legalism? Is it a question of fulfilling both?

Fasting and tithing, even more so giving away our possessions to the poor, go against the grain. Society might encourage us to diet in order to be healthier or more attractive, but often there is a consumer agenda hidden there, too—buy this product and it will make you more beautiful. For the Pharisee, doing these things made him look and feel good. He was attempting to buy his way into heaven by doing them and he does not even mind everyone else knowing it. Jesus' reaction does not mean that fasting and tithing are bad in themselves, however. Pope John Paul II expressed the link this way ('Fasting and solidarity: Pontifical messages for Lent', Pontifical Council Cor Unum, 1991):

Within the same family, can some members eat their fill while their brothers and sisters are excluded from the table? To think of those who suffer is not enough. In this time of Lent, conversion of heart calls us to add fasting to our prayer, and to fill with God's love the efforts that the demands of justice towards neighbour inspire us to make.

We often contrast faith and works. Can fasting encourage us to think about how these are linked?

HARRY SMART

To eat or not to eat...

So Cornelius said, 'Four days ago I was fasting until this hour; and at the ninth hour I prayed in my house, and behold, a man stood before me in bright clothing, and said, "Cornelius, your prayer has been heard, and your alms are remembered in the sight of God. Send therefore to Joppa and call Simon here, whose surname is Peter... When he comes, he will speak to you."'

Cornelius was a centurion, greatly respected by the Jewish community, described as fearing God and giving alms. He is shown here as having fasted as part of his prayer. In many other translations, his fasting is not included, but this may be because the translators felt that prayer inevitably included fasting.

Peter had been a fisherman and an observant Jew. Encountering Jesus totally changed his life and further changes were to come. His dream of clean and unclean food with the command to 'kill and eat' disturbs him. He has always observed the law regarding food. More is at stake than food, however. Peter responds to Cornelius' request by laying out what would be normal practice: 'You know how unlawful it is for a Jewish man to keep company or go to one of another nation' (v. 28). This may be a dramatic exaggeration—Jews would have had regular contact with Gentiles—but the main point is, 'God has shown me that I should not call any man common or unclean' (v. 28).

As we have seen, Cornelius has been fasting and, in a story about eating with others, he too has been thinking about who he might eat with. There are times to refrain from eating or restrict what we eat. Peter does not decide immediately to eat unclean food. He recognises the deeper truth: something new is coming to birth, a society where people are not demarcated as unclean.

I enjoy tradition. It can speak about deep psychological truth and the experiences of others apart from ourselves, but Peter realises he has to have the courage to question his own dearly held practices.

When does tradition inspire us? When do we need to challenge it in the interest of justice?

HARRY SMART

Listening to the Spirit

While they were worshipping the Lord and fasting, the Holy Spirit said, 'Set apart for me Barnabas and Saul for the work to which I have called them.' Then after fasting and praying they laid their hands on them and sent them off.

The people of the early church had many decisions to make that would be key to the core nature and future of Christianity. Barnabas and Peter have been responsible for major changes. Peter's acceptance of the centurion Cornelius heralded the opening of Christianity to Gentiles. Barnabas' courage in introducing Saul, still fresh from persecuting followers of the Way, to the apostles led to huge theological development within Christian thought and teaching.

Barnabas and Saul had been teaching in Antioch for over a year and were sent out to take money to their fellow Christians in Judea. Some of the Christians of Antioch, described as 'prophets and teachers', decide to appoint Paul and Barnabas to go on a missionary journey through Cyprus to Iconium and, eventually, back to Antioch. In Iconium, non-Christians in particular are addressed by the apostles.

The prophets and teachers had a hard decision to make. They needed to be open to the Spirit's promptings, and they prepared to be so by praying and fasting. Fasting seems to have been a natural activity for the prophets. Moses and Elijah in their fasting were preparing for the coming of new things—the kindling or rekindling of faith. The leaders in Antioch seem to have been open to something similar. Perhaps the events of the last year had led them to anticipate it.

What happens next is not the rather bloody action and change that Elijah heralded, nor the coming of the commandments as Moses revealed them, but a new action—the declaration of God's love for all people. The Christians of Antioch fasted, giving up their normal diet and eating something more restricted and simplified because they needed to be open to what was essential, life-changing and new. From them the gospel travelled far.

What is the Holy Spirit causing me to hunger for?

HARRY SMART

Enforced fasting

Just before daybreak, Paul urged all of them to take some food, saying, 'Today is the fourteenth day that you have been in suspense and
remaining without food, having eaten nothing. Therefore I urge you to
take some food, for it will help you survive, for none of you will lose a
hair from your heads.' After he had said this, he took bread; and giving
thanks to God in the presence of all, he broke it and began to eat.

Paul was taken prisoner and, because of his Roman citizenship, he
was transferred to Rome by ship. Paul had, in fact, challenged the
Roman authorities to decide on his fate. The ship was caught in a
wild storm. This storm has great symbolic importance. At a point of
development of the early church, one of its main leaders is taken to
the centre of the known world, the melting pot of cultures and
authority in the Roman Empire. The storm can be seen as an image
of this conflict and struggle, the groanings and labour pains of creation that Paul writes about in Romans, chapter 8.

The fast that those on the ship were forced to undergo was not one
chosen willingly, but we have seen that fasting is often related to
waiting and hoping for something new. Now, the sailors are waiting
for the stilling of a storm that is far greater than anything the disciples experienced on the Sea of Galilee.

As a hospital chaplain, I often visit patients who are to have 'nil
by mouth'. They might be asked to fast for several hours before an
operation. Those hours can be difficult for patients, who become
thirsty, bored, hungry and may need the comfort of food. I have had
conversations with people who are keen cooks and fantasise about
food when kept on a drip. Once, for a woman who was not able to
eat or drink, I held a Communion service in which there was neither
physical bread nor wine.

Paul breaks the fast during a great storm. Shortly afterwards, the
ship runs aground and all aboard come safely to the island of Malta.

---

*Many people are forced to be without food. How can we and they come
to know and share the hope of God's kingdom and healing love?*

HARRY SMART

Are we nearly there yet?

Why do you submit to regulations, 'Do not handle, Do not taste, Do not touch'? All these regulations refer to things that perish with use; they are simply human commands and teachings. These have indeed an appearance of wisdom in promoting self-imposed piety, humility, and severe treatment of the body, but they are of no value in checking self-indulgence.

Extreme religious practices can seem attractive and powerful. The Colossians have encountered the expectations of those who believed that true faith required abasement and self-hatred. Jesus warns of those who travel across land and sea in pursuit of a convert and make their state worse than it was before. Judging oneself and others by legalistic measures can lead to a sense of hopelessness or spiralling self-contempt. The letter to the Colossians counters this with regular appeals to the readers to retain a sense of hope. This is a hope not just for the Colossians but also for the whole of creation. Hope has been 'bearing fruit among yourselves from the day you heard it and truly comprehended the grace of God' (1:6).

Fasting, in its Lent form, is sometimes confused with self-punishment. Not only does this encourage a sense of God as being punishing and cruel but it also lets us give up too easily. Fear might encourage us to change, but we do so with resentment. Doing something with hope and with a sense of being loved by God provides a far deeper motivation. Perhaps that is why Jesus encourages us to fast and look happy at the same time! Controlled fasting or limiting your diet can be a way of expressing the tension of living between hope and mourning. We human beings are compromised and partial, living with our weaknesses and failures as well as our strengths. Living in an attitude of deep fasting does not reflect our human reality before God, but neither does feasting, as though the kingdom is already here in its fullness.

Lord, if I am in a race, you are the goal and the race track, too.
Encourage me so that I can be inspired by hope for you and
a fuller knowledge of your love for me.

HARRY SMART

'Don't it always seem to go...'

Meanwhile the disciples were urging him, 'Rabbi, eat something.' But he said to them, 'I have food to eat that you do not know about.'

Fasting seems to represent a willingness to wait in expectation. From Anna in the temple to Paul on the boat on his long voyage to Rome, fasting is about preparing for fulfilment. Fasting is a refusal to be short-changed, a desire for good and nourishing food, rather than acceptance of the food of captivity, food obtained unjustly or cruelly.

During the time that I have been writing these notes, I have sat with several people who are to have 'nil by mouth'. As mentioned, this is when a patient is not to eat because it will interfere with the medication or surgery he or she is to receive. Sometimes those who are nil by mouth are seriously ill and being unable to eat can express the isolation from the everyday world that they are experiencing. I have visited many who have been away from home for days or weeks, unable to spend time in their familiar environments or with those they love. They are disconnected from their normal lives. I often ask patients what they are looking forward to about when they will be back at home and what keeps them going. Often, seeing relatives and friends is the main answer. Going out in the sun is another, even if people cannot garden any more. For some, the prospect of being able to go to their own homes is small or they may be terminally ill.

The other day, I was sitting with a patient who was not able to eat and could hardly communicate. She was very weak. We were stripped of easy conversation. I was only able to hold her hand. In that time of being present together, there was a sense of going beyond what we would normally consider to be vital. Knowing ourselves as being loved is the ultimate answer to fasting. Perhaps there the glimpse of God begins to be unveiled so we have clearer sight of it.

'They shall not hunger or thirst' (Isaiah 49:10). Who would you most like to break your fast with? What does your glimpse of God reveal?

HARRY SMART

My favourite scriptures

It is not easy when you are asked to share your favourite Bible passages and stories. Where to begin? There are so many! It is especially difficult when you are asked to narrow it down to eleven.

I make no apology for riding a few personal hobby horses here. I have focused particularly on stories of women, as they are the ones who are often ignored in sermons, Sunday school and pretty much anywhere the Bible is read and interpreted. Many readers and hearers will have never even heard of some of these women before, so I think it is only fair to rescue them from obscurity. We women have few enough spiritual role models as it is.

Nor do I apologise for getting a bit 'political' at times. The Bible is essentially the story of a small, vulnerable nation (but one more ethically and spiritually advanced than many of its neighbours) trying to survive in the midst of war and ever-shifting political alliances, with nearby superpowers rising, then falling and being replaced by their successors. This collection of books has many things to say about how we treat our neighbours, how we form communities and how to act if we rise to a position of power. What is that if not political?

Of course, I have included one or two stories that encourage and soothe me in times of distress or when God seems distant or even absent. I have also chosen some that challenge me to follow Jesus more closely and take more risks in my life as his disciple. First of all, as a pointer to how I am approaching the other ten, I have started with a couple of verses that, for me, are the foundation stone for how we read the Bible in the light of Jesus, which, as we are Christians, is the best way to read it.

VERONICA ZUNDEL

Jesus at the centre

Long ago God spoke to our ancestors in many and various ways by the prophets, but in these last days he has spoken to us by a Son, whom he appointed heir of all things, through whom he also created the worlds. He is the reflection of God's glory and the exact imprint of God's very being, and he sustains all things by his powerful word.

What tools do you use to interpret the Bible? We are all interpreters, whether we know it or not. You may read the work of Bible scholars or rely on preachers to interpret the Bible for you or ask the Holy Spirit to help you individually or study together in a group. Some look for challenge in the scriptures or encouragement or sound doctrine. All these methods are fine, but I think they can all lead us astray if we do not pay attention to this crucial verse. The most important word is in the first sentence: 'but'. Not 'and', but 'but'. It links to what Jesus says in the Sermon on the Mount, 'You have heard that it was said to those of ancient times... But I say to you' (Matthew 5:21–22).

The Anabaptist movement, to which I belong, practises a 'Jesus-centred hermeneutic' ('hermeneutic' simply means a way of interpreting). We believe that God's revelation in Jesus changes how we understand all the rest of scripture. For instance, the way Jesus continually broke the sabbath rules, putting people before principles, changes the way we see sabbath observance. His touching of 'unclean' people—lepers, the dead, haemorrhaging women—changes how we see what God counts as 'pure'. Perhaps most importantly of all, his command to love enemies should change our attitude to violence, at both a personal and a state level.

Put simply, if an interpretation does not conform to how Jesus spoke and acted, it is not Christian. God can still speak to us in 'many and various ways' (Hebrews 1:1) via the scriptures, but every understanding must be tested against Jesus' life, death and resurrection.

'You search the scriptures because you think that in them you have eternal life... Yet you refuse to come to me to have life' (John 5:39–40).

VERONICA ZUNDEL

The living Word

In the beginning was the Word, and the Word was with God, and the Word was God. He was in the beginning with God. All things came into being through him, and without him not one thing came into being. What has come into being in him was life, and the life was the light of all people. The light shines in the darkness, and the darkness did not overcome it.

Every Advent in my childhood, my (non-Christian) family would go to the candlelit Anglo-German carol service in the then brand new Coventry Cathedral. Readings were in English and German—the two languages I grew up with—and included this passage, so it is one of the first Bible passages I encountered and I have always loved it, not least for its wonderful poetry.

One thing it tells us is that Jesus is the true Word of God. Yes, the Bible is where we learn to know Jesus, but whenever we place anything in the Bible above the revelation of God in Jesus, we are making a grave mistake: 'for the letter kills, but the Spirit gives life' (2 Corinthians 3:6). 'The Bible says' means nothing if we do not live in the love of Christ.

Particularly important is the way the passage ends: 'And the Word became flesh and lived among us, and we have seen his glory, the glory as of a father's only son, full of grace and truth' (John 1:14). Jesus is no longer with us in the flesh, but we are the body of Christ and, in us, the Word becomes flesh again. 'Christ in you, the hope of glory' (Colossians 1:27b). The Catholic writer Richard Rohr notes, 'When God gives of God's self, one of two things happens: either flesh is inspirited or Spirit is enfleshed… God's will is always incarnation' (*The Naked Now*).

So our actions and words are ultimately the actions and words of Jesus and they need to be consistent with the spirit of Jesus. We can only manage this if his Holy Spirit lives in us.

'It is no longer I who live, but it is Christ who lives in me'
(Galatians 2:20). Pray that this may be true of you.

VERONICA ZUNDEL

129

Streams in the desert

Caleb said, 'Whoever attacks Kiriath-sepher and takes it, to him I will give my daughter Achsah as wife.' Othniel son of Kenaz, the brother of Caleb, took it; and he gave him his daughter Achsah as wife. When she came to him, she urged him to ask her father for a field. As she dismounted from her donkey, Caleb said to her, 'What do you want?' She said to him, 'Give me a present; since you have set me in the land of the Negeb, give me springs of water as well.' So Caleb gave her the upper springs and the lower springs.

Today we are moving away from looking at how the Bible 'works' and focusing on particular Bible stories. This one was special to me in my long years of singleness, which often felt like a desert (I finally got married on my 36th birthday). For much of that time I worked at home and so it might be that I would not speak to anyone for days.

Achsah, like many women around the world today, has no choice about whom she marries; she is handed to her cousin as a battle prize. Not only that, but all she has for a dowry is land in the Negeb (now Negev) desert. Also, her new husband seems reluctant to ask his father-in-law for land with water, so she has to go herself (note how she goes on a donkey, not a warhorse, though her soldier husband probably had some; she is assertive but not aggressive). She gets her wish.

In my 'desert' of aloneness, God often sent me 'springs of water': an unexpected call from a friend, an opportunity to go out for the evening, a welcome letter. (It was long before email or Facebook!) Like Caleb, Jesus often asked people, 'What do you want?' even when it was obvious. Is God asking us the same question? We may not know quite what we want until we ask.

God is not a vending machine, producing goodies if we put in the right prayers, but is a loving parent and loving parents want to give their children gifts.

'You do not have, because you do not ask' (James 4:2b).

VERONICA ZUNDEL

Daughters are heirs

Then the daughters of Zelophehad came forward... The names of his daughters were: Mahlah, Noah, Hoglah, Milcah, and Tirzah. They stood before Moses, Eleazar the priest, the leaders, and all the congregation... and they said, 'Our father died in the wilderness... and he had no sons. Why should the name of our father be taken away from his clan because he had no son? Give to us a possession among our father's brothers.' Moses brought their case before the Lord. And the Lord spoke to Moses, saying: 'The daughters of Zelophehad are right... you shall indeed let them possess an inheritance among their father's brothers and pass the inheritance of their father on to them.'

Traditionally, the British crown passed to the firstborn son of the reigning monarch, unless that monarch had only daughters. Only a few years ago, the law was changed so that the firstborn inherits regardless of gender. The people of Israel arrived at complete equality in inheritance law around 3000 years earlier!

I suspect few of us have heard of Zelophehad's daughters, but their 'campaign' was groundbreaking. Owning land and being able to pass it to your offspring was vital then, not only economically but also spiritually, for the land was the guarantee that God had chosen this people. Mahlah and her sisters were making a bold request, but Moses, listening to God, recognised the justice of their claim—and extended it to all daughters.

I have a personal 'test' that I apply to renewal movements in the church. If a movement raises the status and participation of women, I think it is a genuine initiative of the Spirit. If not, I am more suspicious. After all, Jesus paid special attention to women, giving them roles they had never had before: evangelist (John 4:39), student of a rabbi (Luke 10:39), witness to the gospel (John 20:18). Also, circumcision is a sign that applies only to men, but baptism is the same for all.

'As many of you as were baptised into Christ have clothed yourselves with Christ. There is no longer Jew or Greek, there is no longer slave or free, there is no longer male and female' (Galatians 3:27–28).

VERONICA ZUNDEL

The kindness of God

The king said, 'Is there anyone remaining of the house of Saul to whom I may show the kindness of God?' Ziba said to the king, 'There remains a son of Jonathan; he is crippled in his feet.'... Then King David sent and brought him from the house of Machir son of Ammiel, at Lo-debar. Mephibosheth son of Jonathan son of Saul came to David, and fell on his face and did obeisance... David said to him, 'Do not be afraid, for I will show you kindness for the sake of your father Jonathan; I will restore to you all the land of your grandfather Saul, and you yourself shall eat at my table always.'

For over 35 years I suffered from recurrent depression, though, thankfully, in the last few years, with help from cognitive behavioural therapy and mindfulness training, I have been able to manage my negative feelings much better. It is hard to get mental illness recognised as a disability, but for many people it is a crippling illness that prevents normal everyday life and work.

We have to read this story in the context of the time, which was that anyone with a disability was barred from Jewish worship (Leviticus 21:16ff). Even someone with a birthmark could not offer sacrifices. That was because disability or disfigurement was seen as a punishment from God, either for those people's own sins or the sins of their parents (John 9:2).

Mephibosheth was a casualty of war, dropped by his nurse as she fled David's army (2 Samuel 4:4). He was also the grandson of David's arch-enemy, Saul. Yet David wants to mend the wounds of war by showing 'the kindness of God' (9:3) to any survivors of Saul's family.

Christians with mental health problems can be reproached by other Christians for not being full of the joy of the Lord, not being 'a good witness', but this story tells me that, however damaged, we can still feast at God's table daily, as Mephibosheth did. Note that David also restored his lands, to give him an independent living. This should make us think about how we support people with disabilities today.

Loving God, show me what it means to feast at your table.

VERONICA ZUNDEL

A revolutionary woman

And Mary said, 'My soul magnifies the Lord, and my spirit rejoices in God my Saviour, for he has looked with favour on the lowliness of his servant. Surely, from now on all generations will call me blessed… He has shown strength with his arm; he has scattered the proud in the thoughts of their hearts. He has brought down the powerful from their thrones, and lifted up the lowly; he has filled the hungry with good things, and sent the rich away empty.'

I am writing this two days before a general election in the UK. I cannot help wondering what would happen to a party that promised in its manifesto to bring down the powerful, lift up the lowly, fill the hungry and send the rich away empty. Sounds a bit revolutionary, does it not?

I see Mary as both the last Old Testament prophet and the first New Testament one. Her subversive prophecy owes a lot to the grateful prayer of Hannah after her son Samuel was born (1 Samuel 2:1–10), but it also foreshadows Jesus' inaugural speech at Nazareth, which we will look at tomorrow. If this is her response to knowing she will bear him, we can hardly suppose she brought him up to be compliant with all authorities and not question the political status quo. She should not really have been surprised when he took off on his own to have a theological discussion with the religious leaders (Luke 2:41–50, especially verse 49).

Mary is far from the pale, submissive damsel often portrayed in art. She was probably only a young teenager when she conceived Jesus, but what a stroppy teenager. I think she is a model for all of us, of whatever gender, to speak out against social injustice. Note, too, that, in the style of what scholars call 'realised eschatology', she talks about this great political reversal as though it has already happened.

'I will pour out my spirit on all flesh; your sons and your daughters shall prophesy… Even on the male and female slaves, in those days, I will pour out my spirit' (Joel 2:28–29). How should we fulfil this promise in the church and society?

VERONICA ZUNDEL

Bad news for the rich?

When he came to Nazareth, where he had been brought up, he went to the synagogue on the sabbath day, as was his custom. He stood up to read, and the scroll of the prophet Isaiah was given to him. He unrolled the scroll and found the place where it was written: 'The Spirit of the Lord is upon me, because he has anointed me to bring good news to the poor. He has sent me to proclaim release to the captives and recovery of sight to the blind, to let the oppressed go free, to proclaim the year of the Lord's favour.'… Then he began to say to them, 'Today this scripture has been fulfilled in your hearing.'

What do you expect when you hear a sermon? Teaching, perhaps, or encouragement or a challenge to think through an issue? What you probably do not expect is an announcement that a new age has begun and the kingdom of God is at hand. All that, too, from the local carpenter's son. No wonder the people's reaction was mixed.

Is good news for the poor inevitably bad news for the rich? On a planet that is reaching the limits of sustainability, I fear it is. We who have much need to accept losses in order for those who have nothing to have enough. Likewise, the release of captives and freedom of the oppressed is bad news for those who captured or oppressed them, as they must surrender their power.

Jesus' 'Nazareth manifesto' owes much to his mother's song of rejoicing that we looked at yesterday. Is it fanciful to think that she sang it to him? He too announced a great reversal—the powerful surrendering power and the rich sharing with the poor. How should this influence our politics and theology? The church has not always been successful at bringing good news to the poor and we can at times be condescending or even exclusive. We need to learn from the one who, 'though he was rich, yet for our sakes he became poor' (2 Corinthians 8:9) and, as one translation of John 1:14 says, 'pitched his tent among us'.

Lord, help me to let go of what I cling to, so I can share it with others.

VERONICA ZUNDEL

Stand tall

Now he was teaching in one of the synagogues on the sabbath. And just then there appeared a woman with a spirit that had crippled her for eighteen years. She was bent over and was quite unable to stand up straight. When Jesus saw her, he called her over and said, 'Woman, you are set free from your ailment.' When he laid his hands on her, immediately she stood up straight and began praising God.

You can tell a lot about someone's mental state by their posture. People who are depressed, disappointed or feel that they do not belong tend to bow their heads and try to take up as little space as possible. Confident people, however, spread out and take all the room they can. To stand up straight is to be on an 'equal footing' with everyone else, to look them in the eye and proclaim your own worth as a human being.

I like the translation of this passage where Jesus says, 'Woman, you are freed from your infirmity' (RSV). Society has often treated women as in some way infirm, the 'weaker sex' (personally, I think Paul's words on this should be rendered as 'the more vulnerable sex'), but Jesus asks this woman to stand tall, to be all she is called to be. Also, in his reply to the synagogue leader who criticises him for healing on the sabbath, he refers to her as 'this daughter of Abraham'—an unprecedentedly honourable title.

What would it take for you to 'stand tall' as a daughter or son of God? We are called to be humble, but not to have no self-esteem. True humility means being able to set aside our rights, but first we need to know that we have them. As I write, a new princess has just been born to the British royal family. But, as commentator Savi Hensman points out, 'every birth [should be] seen as royal', as we are all made in the image of God, the true monarch.

'I will rejoice in Jerusalem… No more shall there be an infant that lives but a few days' (Isaiah 65:19–20).

VERONICA ZUNDEL

Friendly enemy aliens?

But now in Christ Jesus you who once were far off have been brought near by the blood of Christ. For he is our peace; in his flesh he has made both groups into one and has broken down the dividing wall, that is, the hostility between us... So he came and proclaimed peace to you who were far off and peace to those who were near; for through him both of us have access in one Spirit to the Father. So then you are no longer strangers and aliens, but you are citizens with the saints and also members of the household of God.

When my parents emigrated to the UK from Vienna, German refugees were called 'enemy aliens', but Austrians, because their country had been annexed by the Nazis, were known as 'friendly enemy aliens'. This always makes me laugh!

One of my favourite sayings is, 'The world is divided into two sorts of people: those who divide it into two sorts of people and those who do not.' Humankind is prone to creating dividing walls: black and white, men and women, East and West, Christians and 'non-Christians'. How would you like to be defined by what you are not?

The writer focuses on how God has broken down the wall dividing the Jews and Gentiles, but he could equally be talking about any other human divisions. Yes, this particular division was broken down in a particular way, by the death and resurrection of Jesus, but if God breaks this down, why would God not want to break down all others? In the USA, immigrants are still labelled 'aliens', but God's desire is to break down this language of otherness and reconcile all humanity—first to God, then to each other.

A poster that hung in the London Mennonite Centre offers a 'modest proposal': 'Let the Christians of the world agree not to kill one another'. If you think about it, it is not all that modest for in a war, how would you know? Our call is more than to make 'enemy aliens' into 'friendly enemy aliens'; it is to turn them into friends.

Whoever is my enemy, Lord, teach me to turn them into my friend.

VERONICA ZUNDEL

What kind of world?

'When the Son of Man comes in his glory, and all the angels with him, then he will sit on the throne of his glory. All the nations will be gathered before him, and he will separate people one from another as a shepherd separates the sheep from the goats, and he will put the sheep at his right hand and the goats at the left. Then the king will say to those at his right hand, "Come, you that are blessed by my Father, inherit the kingdom prepared for you from the foundation of the world; for I was hungry and you gave me food, I was thirsty and you gave me something to drink, I was a stranger and you welcomed me, I was naked and you gave me clothing, I was sick and you took care of me, I was in prison and you visited me."'

I confess, this used to be one of my least favourite scripture passages. Whenever I read it, I feared I would be among the 'goats' who failed to recognise Jesus in the poor, the sick, hungry, stranger. I knew I lived a privileged life and did not feel that I had done all I could to care for the needy.

Then, one day, I noticed something. This parable is not just about individuals: 'All the *nations* will be gathered before him' (my italics)! It is also about what kind of society we want to build together. Jesus is not requiring individuals here to kill themselves trying to meet every need. He is asking us to work together to foster a nation, a world where the poorest and most vulnerable are noticed and cared for. How are we doing on implementing this?

We know that we are not saved by our acts of generosity, but a salvation that does not result in acts of generosity does not look much like the sort of salvation Jesus talks about. The story goes that an earnest Christian asked an old Amish man if he was saved. The Amish man replied, 'See that man over there? He is my neighbour. He will tell you if I am saved.'

What can I and my church do to foster a world that cares for the weakest?

VERONICA ZUNDEL

All things new

Then I saw a new heaven and a new earth; for the first heaven and the first earth had passed away... And I saw the holy city, the new Jerusalem, coming down out of heaven from God... And I heard a loud voice from the throne saying, 'See, the home of God is among mortals. He will dwell with them... he will wipe every tear from their eyes. Death will be no more; mourning and crying and pain will be no more, for the first things have passed away.' And the one who was seated on the throne said, 'See, I am making all things new.'

Forty years ago, my only brother killed himself after nine years in and out of psychiatric wards. He was 27, I was 22 and it was the term before my finals. I found myself supporting my parents when I needed support myself. Then and many times since, this passage has been a great comfort to me.

When someone dies, we speak of them having 'gone to a better place', but this passage says nothing about us 'going to heaven'. Rather, it portrays heaven coming to us, to a transformed earth, where God lives among us. Also, he is not a God who comes to condemn (see John 3:17) but one like a mother comforting her child, wiping away every tear and destroying every sorrow. Who would not want to respond to such a God? I believe we need not threaten hell to get people to believe in Jesus; we simply need to communicate the love of God as fully as we can.

What about the world in the meantime? As God made it and wants to save it, should we not be making every effort to make it as good a world as we can? With the help of the Holy Spirit, we should aim for the welfare of all and fight poverty, inequality, violence, discrimination. It is worth studying the phrase 'all things' in the New Testament. You will see that God's plan leaves nothing and no one out.

'The Lord... is patient with you, not wanting any to perish, but all to come to repentance' (2 Peter 3:9).

VERONICA ZUNDEL

Reading *New Daylight* in a group

SALLY WELCH

Some *New Daylight* readers may like to study in small groups, to enable conversation and the sharing of insights. With this in mind, here are some ideas for discussion starters within a study group. Some of the questions can be applied to any set of contributions within this issue; others are specific to certain sets of readings. There are no right or wrong answers: these questions are simply to enable a group to engage in conversation.

General discussion starters

- What do you think is the main idea or theme of the author in each series? Do you think they succeeded in communicating it to you, or were you more interested in the side issues?

- Have you had any experience of the issues that are raised in the study? How have they affected your life?

- What evidence does the author use to support their ideas? Do they use personal observations and experiences, facts, or quotations from other authorities? Which appeals to you most?

- Does the author make a 'call to action'? Is that call realistic and achievable? Do you think their ideas will work in the secular world?

- Can you identify specific passages that struck you personally—as interesting, profound, difficult to understand or illuminating?

Feasting in the New Testament (Penelope Wilcock)

Penelope helps us to follow the thread of feasting and celebration through the New Testament. Does this help you to see the books within it as a more integrated whole? Has the series changed your views on parties and celebrations?

The character of David (Michael Mitton)

Michael's contribution studies the character of David using the evidence of the Bible. Does this approach appeal to you? Has this study given you new insights into David's nature and his relationship with God? How has it helped you to reflect on your own relationship with God?

Reflective question: 'Facing death' by Rachel Boulding

Rachel Boulding has written a very moving and personal account of her experience of terminal cancer. What has it been like to share the journey with Rachel? What is her attitude to death, and is it the same as your own? Has the series caused you to think differently about death?

Author profile: Harry Smart

Revd Harry Smart is a new contributor to *New Daylight*. Editor **Sally Welch** asked him to talk about his work and his writing.

How long have you been an Anglican priest, and what inspired you to seek ordination?

I was ordained 21 years ago and served my curacy in Thirsk and in Sheffield. It was Jesus' radical challenge, combined with his compassion, that first attracted me. I wanted to deal with questions about the meaning of life and how we live it, and ministry has brought opportunities both to question and to celebrate.

You tell us that you are a mental health chaplain. Can you describe what your job involves?

I was a mental health chaplain for over 15 years. I'm now in general hospital chaplaincy. I love working with people and helping others when they confront questions and challenges to their lives. When we become ill we ask questions about what is fundamental to our lives, what keeps us going. I am able to be present at such times. Sometimes that will be within an explicit religious context, but sometimes patients will say, 'We haven't discussed God, but he's been here all the time, hasn't he?'

What are the best and worst things about being a hospital chaplain?

Our ministry is often at the edge of life—being with parents at the death of a child, or with someone nearing the end of their own life. That can be hard, but often there is a sense of helping people face the situation with dignity and respect. I love listening to people's stories, and helping them to discover a sense of resurrection.

How do you use mindfulness and labyrinths in your work?

I became interested in labyrinths through Lincoln diocese's work several years ago. They are a powerful symbol of our life's pilgrimage. I used them within my mental health work, enabling people to see where God was working in their lives, or to feel less stuck in their illness. Mindfulness is helpful in the NHS context, where stress can be very great for staff; having a moment to recharge and review things can be reinvigorating.

How did you get involved in writing for New Daylight *and how are you finding the experience of writing Bible study notes?*

I was asked to write for *New Daylight*, having spoken about my work with labyrinths and mental health. I have very much enjoyed my experience: it has given me a reason to explore themes and passages I haven't looked at before, and the brevity of each daily section means that you have to be focused and clear.

Which spiritual writers have influenced you and in what ways?

Dietrich Bonhoeffer and Thomas Merton have been important influences in my life. Bonhoeffer's courage, and the way he linked theology and practice in Nazi Germany, challenge me not to let my faith become too easygoing or theoretical. Thomas Merton's mysticism is based on an appreciation of creation and coming closer to God.

You live and work in Lincolnshire. What is that like?

The county, especially north Lincolnshire, is perhaps a bit neglected: it's seen as 'out of the way' or very industrial. It's beautiful countryside here, people are very welcoming, and there's a great depth of history which is quite tangible.

Do you have an unfulfilled wish or ambition?

I'd like to write a book reflecting on my experiences, or a novel.

One final question: what would you like your tombstone to say?

I'd like to be remembered as a good priest, a good friend and as someone who reflected on life.

An extract from
The Recovery of Hope

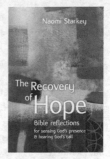

In her new book, **Naomi Starkey** brings together a
selection of her own *New Daylight* readings along
with some newly written poems of reflection. The
following extract introduces the story of Jonah.

Bible stories rediscovered: Jonah

Along with Noah and the ark, Jonah and the
whale is one of the best-known Old Testament stories. It is such a
small but perfectly formed narrative, with fast-paced action, snappy
dialogue, dramatic shifts in scene and, above all, that monstrous
sea creature rearing up from the deep to save the (anti-)hero at the
eleventh hour.

Jonah, the most reluctant of prophets, also appears in 2 Kings
14:25, where he is identified as coming 'from Gathhepher'. Jesus
mentions 'the sign of Jonah' in Matthew 12:39–41 and 16:4, as well
as Luke 11:29–32. In the first of the passages in Matthew, he draws a
comparison between Jonah's sojourn in the 'belly of the sea monster'
and the three days and nights that 'the Son of Man' will spend 'in the
heart of the earth'.

'Did it really happen, though?' some may ask. That may not be a
particularly helpful question in relation to this story.

Some might stubbornly argue that God can do anything he likes,
including providing piscatorial rescue services. What is at the heart
of the adventures of Jonah, however, is not a question of historicity
(or lack of it), but what we learn about God and humanity.

Commentators tend to describe Jonah in disparaging terms and he
is seldom held up as a good example of prophetic witness, but, in fact,
Jonah is no worse—and, in many ways, a good deal braver—than the
rest of us. We should not feel superior to him, but acknowledge how,
like us, he fails and fails and fails again, yet God uses him to achieve
a work so amazing that Jonah struggles to comprehend it.

Like Jonah, we can be humbled to find that, in God's mercy and
grace, we can still play some small part in building his kingdom.

No escape

But the Lord hurled a great wind upon the sea, and such a mighty storm came upon the sea that the ship threatened to break up. Then the mariners were afraid, and each cried to his god... Jonah, meanwhile, had gone down into the hold of the ship and had lain down, and was fast asleep... The sailors said to one another, 'Come, let us cast lots, so that we may know on whose account this calamity has come upon us.' So they cast lots, and the lot fell on Jonah. Then they said to him '... What is this that you have done!' For the men knew that he was fleeing from the presence of the Lord, because he had told them so. (Jonah 1:4–5, 7–8, 10, abridged)

Have you ever been in a small boat on a stormy sea? Even if the wind has died down, the swell can stay heavy for hours and we may fear a sudden rogue wave swamping us. The sailors here face such a 'great wind' and 'mighty storm' that all hope seems lost. If you have not already done so, read this passage in full so as to appreciate the narrator's skill in evoking the scene, the desperate emotional state of the crew mirroring the tempest raging around them.

The sleep of Jonah has been characterised on the one hand as smug somnolence and, on the other, as exhaustion, the depressed mental state of a man who has cut his ties to his old life, including trying to run away from his God. Perhaps what he feels is simply relief; he hopes that he has escaped after all. Despite the fearful sea crossing to be endured, new opportunities may be opening ahead.

Then his secret is discovered. With horrible inevitability, the 'lot' picks him out as the cause of the tempest. Jonah is about to learn just how inescapable God is—and also how compassionate—but his journey will take him literally through very deep waters first. Sometimes for us, too, life gets a whole lot worse before we sense any hint of the skies starting to clear.

REFLECTION

O hear us when we cry to Thee for those in peril on the sea!

WILLIAM WHITING (1860)

Naomi Starkey is a full-time ordained minister in the Church in Wales, living on the Llyn Peninsula in North Wales. From 1997 to 2015 she was a commissioning editor for BRF as well as editing *New Daylight* and *Quiet Spaces* over a number of years.

Recommended reading

KAREN LAISTER and ESTHER TAYLOR

God's Daughters
Loved, held, accepted, enough

HANNAH FYTCHE

pb, 9781841014095, £6.99

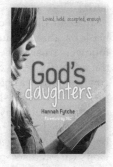

'Do you ever feel like you're not good enough for other people and they will never love or accept you?' Hannah Fytche is only too aware of these feelings and of having to grow up in a culture where there are enormous pressures on young women.

It was her encounter with a passage from 1 Kings 19 that enabled Hannah to see God in a different way and understand that 'God doesn't want us to live craving love and fearing failure when he already loves us and forgives our mistakes'. Hannah explores six issues that young women face today: school, image, friends, family, church and our personal relationship with God.

This book is a must for any Christian teenage girl who is working through those issues of identity and value. Written when Hannah was a teenager, this book provides insights into this critical stage of life and faith development.

Hilda of Whitby
A spirituality for now

RAY SIMPSON

pb, 9781841017280, £7.99

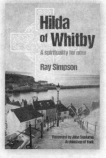

Finding strength in dark times is a challenge we all face, but the power of St Hilda of Whitby—an Anglo-Saxon who lived in a troubled and violent era, among warring pagan tribes—is a testimony to the potential of struggles, and the importance of embracing God during hardship. Published in celebration of the 1400th anniversary of Hilda's birth, this awe-inspiring book is a testimony to the importance of courage, adversity and, above all, faith.

In light of this, one of the most commanding messages in this book is the absolute importance of receptivity. Hilda and her followers trusted the signs they found around them and encouraged the gifts they received, whether they were the songs of Caedmon (a cowherd who was blessed with heavenly music) or the dream Hilda's mother had while she was pregnant, prophesying the role that her daughter would play.

It can be hard to have faith in the insubstantial, in fleeting dreams, but this book testifies to the wonders experienced by surrendering to God's care and accepting him into every part of life.

The Apple of His Eye
Discovering God's loving purpose for each one of us

BRIDGET PLASS

pb, 9781841010885, £7.99

Indeed we are all redeemed by God's love, but *The Apple of his Eye* by Bridget Plass highlights that blessing—the incredible love that he has for each and every one of us. An exploration of Bible passages, this book explores a simple, life-rattling idea: that Jesus delights in us all, that we are more loved than we can understand, and that we are all children of God.

The grace of this love is absolute, and by understanding the words of Jesus we can create lives that praise the glory of God.

Servant Ministry

A portrait of Christ and a pattern for his followers

TONY HORSFALL

pb, 9780857460882, £7.99

Celebrating the glory of God and stepping up to the challenge of worship can be difficult at times. Being a servant of the Lord, and understanding what servanthood means, can appear complex despite its simplicity. This book by Tony Horsfall refreshingly clarifies the role that believers can have in the work of the church, and the power entrusted to us as children of God.

Servant Ministry offers a guided exposition of the first 'Servant Song' in Isaiah 42:1–9, and illustrates what it really means to be a servant—the highs, the lows, and the grace that the position brings.

Deep Calls to Deep

Spiritual formation in the hard places of life

TONY HORSFALL

pb, 9781841017310, £7.99

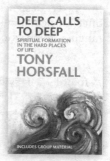

Is there a positive purpose to suffering? The reality of pain, loss and grief is unavoidable, as much a part of life as the beautiful joys. These challenges shape our world, and the struggle often impacts our spiritual growth, harshness and difficulty transforming our spiritual lives. In this book Tony Horsfall postulates that suffering is an inescapable part of the journey to God, and that the seemingly senseless difficulties we face are opportunities for transformation.

Analysing the Psalms of Lament, this book offers a compass to finding God in the hardest of times and being equipped spiritually with the right tools.

80 Creative Prayer Ideas
A resource for church and group use

CLAIRE DANIEL

pb, 9781841016887, £8.99

Prayer can be a source of wonder and joy and enlightenment, but sometimes it can be difficult to carve out a moment dedicated to prayer, to fully embrace the power of what is underway and be entirely in the moment. These 80 prayer ideas are a magnificent resource, creatively bestowing the gift of prayer for the use of churches and groups, so as to magnify the experience and reach out to God in simple but meaningful ways.

This is a book to be celebrated. The act of writing a love letter to God, of praying with water, of using broken pots of clay—these are all linked to higher messages and brought into focus with Bible reflections that enable the thanksgiving, reflection and clarity gifted by prayer. Designed for adults of all ages, these imaginative prayers offer a celebration of God's love, and are made with simple props ranging from stationery to biscuits.

To order a copy of any of these books, please use the order form on pages 149–150. BRF books are also available from your local Christian bookshop or from **www.brfonline.org.uk**.

BRF PUBLICATIONS ORDER FORM

To order our resources online, please visit **www.brfonline.org.uk**

Please send me the following book(s):	Quantity	Price	Total
417 0 **The Recovery of Hope** Naomi Starkey	_____	£8.99	_____
409 5 **God's Daughters** Hannah Fytche	_____	£6.99	_____
728 0 **Hilda of Whitby** Ray Simpson	_____	£7.99	_____
088 5 **The Apple of His Eye** Bridget Plass	_____	£7.99	_____
088 2 **Servant Ministry** Tony Horsfall	_____	£7.99	_____
731 0 **Deep Calls to Deep** Tony Horsfall	_____	£7.99	_____
688 7 **80 Creative Prayer Ideas** Claire Daniel	_____	£8.99	_____
428 6 **Encountering the Risen Christ** Mark Bradford	_____	£7.99	_____
420 0 **Believe in Miracles** Carmel Thomason	_____	£7.99	_____
427 9 **Postcards from Heaven** Ellie Hart	_____	£7.99	_____
379 1 **Messy Prayer** Jane Leadbetter	_____	£6.99	_____
415 6 **Messy Hospitality** Lucy Moore	_____	£9.99	_____
413 2 **The Gift of Years** (Bible reflections)	_____	£2.50	_____
Quiet Spaces FREE sample copy	_____	£0.00	_____

Total cost of books £ _____

Donation £ _____

Postage and packing (*see overleaf*) £ _____

TOTAL £ _____

Please complete the payment details below and return with the appropriate payment to: BRF, 15 The Chambers, Vineyard, Abingdon OX14 3FE

Title _____ First name/initials _____ Surname _____

Address _____

_____ Postcode _____

Telephone _____ Email _____

Total enclosed £ _____ (cheques should be made payable to 'BRF')

Please charge my Visa ☐ Mastercard ☐ Maestro ☐ with £ _____

Card no. ☐☐☐☐ ☐☐☐☐ ☐☐☐☐ ☐☐☐☐

Expiry date ☐☐ ☐☐ Security code ☐☐☐

Issue no. (Maestro only) ☐☐☐☐

Signature (essential if paying by credit card/Maestro) _____

POSTAGE AND PACKING CHARGES				
Order value	UK	Europe	Economy (Surface)	Standard (Air)
Under £7.00	£1.25	£3.00	£3.50	£5.50
£7.00–£29.99	£2.25	£5.50	£6.50	£10.00
£30.00 & over	FREE	Prices on request		

brf Transforming Lives and Communities

BRF is a charity that is passionate about making a difference through the Christian faith. We want to see lives and communities transformed through our creative programmes and resources for individuals, churches and schools. We are doing this by resourcing:

- **Christian growth and understanding of the Bible.** Through our Bible reading notes, books, digital resources, Quiet Days and other events, we're resourcing individuals, groups and leaders in churches for their own spiritual journey and for their ministry.

- **Church outreach in the local community.** BRF is the home of three programmes that churches are embracing to great effect as they seek to engage with their local communities: Messy Church, Who Let The Dads Out? and The Gift of Years.

- **Teaching Christianity in primary schools.** Our Barnabas in Schools team is working with primary-aged children and their teachers, enabling them to explore Christianity creatively within the school curriculum.

- **Children's and family ministry.** Through our Barnabas in Churches and Faith in Homes websites and published resources, we're working with churches and families, enabling children under 11, and the adults working with them, to explore Christianity creatively and bring the Bible alive.

Do you share our vision?

Sales of our books and Bible reading notes cover the cost of producing them. However, our other programmes are funded primarily by donations, grants and legacies. If you share our vision, would you help us to transform even more lives and communities? Your prayers and financial support are vital for the work that we do.

- You could support BRF's ministry with a one-off gift or regular donation (using the response form on page 153).
- You could consider making a bequest to BRF in your will (page 152).
- You could encourage your church to support BRF as part of your church's giving to home mission—perhaps focusing on a specific area of our ministry, or a particular member of our Barnabas team.
- Most important of all, you could support BRF with your prayers.

The difference a gift in your Will can make

Gifts left in Wills don't need to be huge to help us make a real difference. Throughout our history, BRF's work has been enabled thanks to the generosity of those who have shared its vision and supported its work by giving both during their lifetime and also through legacy gifts. All have helped BRF in its mission to transform lives and communities through the Christian faith.

One of the fastest growing areas of BRF is Messy Church. Messy Church reaches people of all ages who have often never set foot in a church before, by being 'church' differently. It is being delivered in a variety of contexts in local communities, including care homes, prisons, inner cities, schools and rural areas. Week by week we are seeing new Messy Churches starting up across the UK and around the globe, and across all major Christian denominations. We estimate that over 500,000 people are attending Messy Church each month.

A legacy gift would help fund the growth, development and sustainability of BRF's Messy Church into the future. Would you consider a legacy gift to help us continue to take this work forward in the decades to come?

For further information about making a gift to BRF in your Will or to discuss how a specific bequest could be used to develop our ministry, please contact Sophie Aldred (Head of Fundraising) or Richard Fisher (Chief Executive) by phone on 01865 319700 or by email at fundraising@brf.org.uk.

Whatever you can do or give, we thank you for your support.

BRF MINISTRY APPEAL RESPONSE FORM

I want to help BRF by funding some of its core ministries. Please use my gift for:

☐ where it is needed most ☐ Barnabas Children's Ministry ☐ Messy Church

☐ Who Let The Dads Out? ☐ The Gift of Years

Please complete all relevant sections of this form and print clearly.

Title _____ First name/initials _____ Surname _____

Address _____

_____ Postcode _____

Telephone _____ Email _____

Regular giving

If you would like to give by direct debit, please tick the box below and fill in details:

☐ I would like to make a regular gift of £ _____ per month / quarter / year
(delete as appropriate) by direct debit. (Please also complete the direct debit
instruction on page 159.)

If you would like to give by standing order, please contact Priscilla Kew:
Tel. 01865 319700 | priscilla.kew@brf.org.uk | or write to her at BRF

One-off donation

Please accept my special gift of:

☐ £10 ☐ £50 ☐ £100 (other) £ _____ by

☐ Cheque / Charity Voucher payable to 'BRF' (delete as appropriate)

☐ Visa / Mastercard / Charity Card (delete as appropriate)

Name on card _____

Card no. ☐☐☐☐ ☐☐☐☐ ☐☐☐☐ ☐☐☐☐

Start date ☐☐☐ Expiry date ☐☐☐

Security code ☐☐☐

Signature _____ Date _____

☐ I would like to leave a legacy to BRF. Please send me further information.

☐ I would like BRF to claim back tax on this gift. (If you tick this box, you will
need to complete the gift aid declaration overleaf.)

**Please return this completed form to: BRF, 15 The Chambers, Vineyard,
Abingdon OX14 3FE**

BRF is a Registered Charity (No. 233280)

GIFT AID DECLARATION

The Bible Reading Fellowship

Please treat as Gift Aid donations all qualifying gifts
of money made

giftaid it

☐ today, ☐ in the past four years, ☐ and in the future.

I confirm I have paid or will pay an amount of Income Tax and/or Capital Gains
Tax for each tax year (6 April to 5 April) that is at least equal to the amount of
tax that all the charities that I donate to will reclaim on my gifts for that tax year.
I understand that other taxes such as VAT or Council Tax do not qualify.
I understand BRF will reclaim 25p of tax on every £1 that I give.

☐ My donation does not qualify for Gift Aid.

Signature _____ Date _____

Notes

1. Please notify BRF if you want to cancel this declaration, change your name
   or home address, or no longer pay sufficient tax on your income and/or
   capital gains.

2. If you pay Income Tax at the higher/additional rate and want to receive the
   additional tax relief due to you, you must include all your Gift Aid donations
   on your Self-Assessment tax return or ask HM Revenue and Customs to adjust
   your tax code.

We like to acknowledge all donations. However, if you do not wish to receive
an acknowledgement, please tick here ☐

How to encourage Bible reading in your church

BRF has been helping individuals connect with the Bible for over 90 years. We want to support churches as they seek to encourage church members into regular Bible reading.

Order a Bible reading resources pack

This pack is designed to give your church the tools to publicise our Bible reading notes. It includes:

- Sample Bible reading notes for your congregation to try.
- Publicity resources, including a poster.
- A church magazine feature about Bible reading notes.

The pack is free, but we welcome a £5 donation to cover the cost of postage. If you require a pack to be sent outside the UK or require a specific number of sample Bible reading notes, please contact us for postage costs. More information about what the current pack contains is available on our website.

How to order and find out more

- Visit www.biblereadingnotes.org.uk/for-churches
- Telephone BRF on 01865 319700 between 9.15 am and 5.30 pm
- Write to us at BRF, 15 The Chambers, Vineyard, Abingdon OX14 3FE

Keep informed about our latest initiatives

We are continuing to develop resources to help churches encourage people into regular Bible reading, wherever they are on their journey. Join our email list at www.biblereadingnotes.org.uk/helpingchurches to stay informed about the latest initiatives that your church could benefit from.

Introduce a friend to our notes

We can send information about our notes and current prices for you to pass on. Please contact us.

NEW DAYLIGHT INDIVIDUAL SUBSCRIPTION FORM

All our Bible reading notes can be ordered online by visiting
www.biblereadingnotes.org.uk/subscriptions

☐ I would like to take out a subscription:

Title _____ First name/initials _____ Surname _____

Address _____

_____ Postcode _____

Telephone _____ Email _____

Please send New Daylight beginning with the September 2016 / January 2017 / May 2017 issue (*delete as appropriate*):

(*please tick box*)	UK	Europe/Economy	Airmail
New Daylight	☐ £16.35	☐ £24.90	☐ £28.20
New Daylight 3-year subscription	☐ £43.20	N/A	N/A
New Daylight DELUXE	☐ £20.70	☐ £33.75	☐ £40.50

Please complete the payment details below and return with the appropriate payment to: BRF, 15 The Chambers, Vineyard, Abingdon OX14 3FE

Total enclosed £ _____ (cheques should be made payable to 'BRF')

Please charge my Visa ☐ Mastercard ☐ Maestro ☐ with £ _____

Card no. ☐☐☐☐ ☐☐☐☐ ☐☐☐☐ ☐☐☐☐

Expiry date ☐☐☐☐   Security code ☐☐☐

Issue no. (Maestro only) ☐☐☐☐

Signature (essential if paying by credit card/Maestro) _____

To set up a direct debit, please also complete the direct debit instruction on page 159 and return it to BRF with this form.

BRF is a Registered Charity (No. 233280)

ND0216

NEW DAYLIGHT GIFT SUBSCRIPTION FORM

☐ I would like to give a gift subscription (please provide both names and addresses):

Title _____ First name/initials _____ Surname _____

Address _____

_____ Postcode _____

Telephone _____ Email _____

Gift subscription name _____

Gift subscription address _____

_____ Postcode _____

Gift message (20 words max. or include your own gift card):

_____

_____

Please send New Daylight beginning with the September 2016 / January 2017 / May 2017 issue (*delete as appropriate*):

(*please tick box*)		UK	Europe/Economy	Airmail
New Daylight		☐ £16.35	☐ £24.90	☐ £28.20
New Daylight 3-year subscription		☐ £43.20	N/A	N/A
New Daylight DELUXE		☐ £20.70	☐ £33.75	☐ £40.50

Please complete the payment details below and return with the appropriate payment to: BRF, 15 The Chambers, Vineyard, Abingdon OX14 3FE

Total enclosed £ _____ (cheques should be made payable to 'BRF')

Please charge my Visa ☐ Mastercard ☐ Maestro ☐ with £ _____

Card no. ☐☐☐☐ ☐☐☐☐ ☐☐☐☐ ☐☐☐☐

Expiry date ☐☐☐☐ Security code ☐☐☐

Issue no. (Maestro only) ☐☐☐☐

Signature (essential if paying by credit card/Maestro) _____

To set up a direct debit, please also complete the direct debit instruction on page 159 and return it to BRF with this form.

DIRECT DEBIT PAYMENT

You can pay for your annual subscription to our Bible reading notes using Direct Debit. You need only give your bank details once, and the payment is made automatically every year until you cancel it. If you would like to pay by Direct Debit, please use the form opposite, entering your BRF account number under 'Reference'.

You are fully covered by the Direct Debit Guarantee:

The Direct Debit Guarantee

- This Guarantee is offered by all banks and building societies that accept instructions to pay Direct Debits.

- If there are any changes to the amount, date or frequency of your Direct Debit, The Bible Reading Fellowship will notify you 10 working days in advance of your account being debited or as otherwise agreed. If you request The Bible Reading Fellowship to collect a payment, confirmation of the amount and date will be given to you at the time of the request.

- If an error is made in the payment of your Direct Debit, by The Bible Reading Fellowship or your bank or building society, you are entitled to a full and immediate refund of the amount paid from your bank or building society.

- If you receive a refund you are not entitled to, you must pay it back when The Bible Reading Fellowship asks you to.

- You can cancel a Direct Debit at any time by simply contacting your bank or building society. Written confirmation may be required. Please also notify us.

The Bible Reading Fellowship

Instruction to your bank or building society to pay by Direct Debit

Please fill in the whole form using a ballpoint pen and return it to:
BRF, 15 The Chambers, Vineyard, Abingdon OX14 3FE

Service User Number: | 5 | 5 | 8 | 2 | 2 | 9 |

Name and full postal address of your bank or building society

To: The Manager	Bank/Building Society
Address	
	Postcode

Name(s) of account holder(s)

Branch sort code

Bank/Building Society account number

Reference

Instruction to your Bank/Building Society

Please pay The Bible Reading Fellowship Direct Debits from the account detailed in this instruction, subject to the safeguards assured by the Direct Debit Guarantee. I understand that this instruction may remain with The Bible Reading Fellowship and, if so, details will be passed electronically to my bank/building society.

Signature(s)

Banks and Building Societies may not accept Direct Debit instructions for some types of account.

ND0216

This page is for your notes.